OTHER TITLES BY
MERRILEE BOYACK

Books

52 Weeks of Fun Family Service
The Parenting Breakthrough
Strangling Your Husband Is Not an Option

Talks on CD

How Do I Change My Husband?
Teaching Your Children to Fly: A Guide to Independence

Toss the Guilt

AND CATCH THE

JY

A Woman's Guide to a Better Life

MERRILEE BOYACK

DESERET
BOOK

SALT LAKE CITY, UTAH

To my husband, Steve, who, anytime I come up with a harebrained idea, says these three wonderful words,

"GO for it!"

You have always cheered me on, and I am grateful.

Library of Congress Cataloging-in-Publication Data

Boyack, Merrilee Browne.
  Toss the guilt and catch the joy : a woman's guide to a better life / Merrilee Boyack.
       p.   cm.
  Includes bibliographical references and index.
  ISBN 978-1-59038-925-6 (pbk.)
  1. Christian women—Religious life.   2. Mormon women—Religious life.
I. Title.
  BV4527.B681 2008
  248.8'43—dc22   2008016105

Printed in the United States of America
Publishers Printing, Salt Lake City, UT

10   9   8   7   6   5   4   3   2   1

Contents

Preface

I was sitting on the third row at a funeral. My husband's grandmother had passed away after a long life. Speaker after speaker extolled the virtues of this good and loving woman, commenting on her wonderful ability to whip up the perfect banana cream pie, her cooking and homemaking skills, the wonderful creations she would produce at the sewing machine, and her constant vigilance of motherhood over her children and grandchildren. My son leaned over to me and whispered in my ear, "Sorry, Mom. They're never gonna say that stuff at your funeral." I gave him a baleful look, and we both snickered.

But as I sat there thinking about my son's words, part of me was sad. It's true—I'm not a great cook. And I tend to do my homemaking duties as fast as I can just to get them over with. I never follow my kids around asking, "Can I get you something?" I'm more likely to holler from the couch, "While you're up, can you grab me something?" So, yes, part of me was wondering if I should give my life a whole lot more effort. Part of me felt guilty.

And then I compared other aspects of my life with this good woman's life. We are very different people. I am most comfortable and happy speaking in front of thousands, while the mere idea would have sent her scurrying out of the room at the speed of light.

She could whip up dinner for twenty in the blink of an eye, while I would be in the fetal position just thinking about it.

So is there room in the kingdom for both of us?

I think so.

But that day I also realized that I wanted to be better at being *me*. At the end of my mortal life's journey, I, too, would be surrounded by those who loved me and whom I loved. And what would be said of my life? What would they say about who I had been and who I had become?

I wanted to be better, and I wanted to live a better life that was motivated by love—not by guilt. I didn't want to be pushed to and fro by feelings of "Gee, I should . . ." or "I'll feel guilty if I don't . . ." or "Well, I'm expected to . . ."

President Gordon B. Hinckley often expressed that same desire. At the end of many general conferences, he would express his desire to be a little bit better. I'd always quip to my family, "Yeah, well, he's a prophet and he's like 99% there! He only has to be a *little* bit better. I've got to be a *lot* better!" But in my heart I was always impressed by his request that we all be a little bit better.

That's what I want. I just want to get up every day and try to be a little bit better. I don't want to get bogged down trying to live my life according to someone else's recipe book. I don't want to get bogged down in guilt. I just want to be walking on my own path each day.

So I invite you on this journey as we walk together. We are all unique, but we can still walk together. I invite you to join me as we toss the guilt and catch the joy!

Feel free to send me an e-mail of your joyful experiences to maboyack@gmail.com or through my Web site at Boyacks.com/Merrilee.

CHAPTER 1

Women of Joy, Not Guilt

I remember the day quite clearly. I had had a rough week caring for my four little boys. It was Saturday. And my sweet husband said to me, "Why don't you go have fun? I'll take care of the kids." I thought that was a stellar idea. I got in the van (which I lovingly call "The Mother Ship") and sat. Where to go? What to do? I sat for a long time.

My organized, serious mind went to work. *Well, I should go get the grocery shopping caught up. I should probably drop by my visiting teachees and take them a treat. I should go to the club and exercise.* Down the list my mind went. And then my fun side spoke up, *You have a whole day! For heaven's sake, go do something fun! You can do anything you want!*

I can't remember what I did that Saturday, but I remember that mental debate quite clearly.

I know I'm not the only one who faces this dilemma. Listen and see if any of these voices sound familiar.

- "A hot bath sounds wonderful right now, but I'd better finish this project for work."
- "I want to go out with my friends, but I need to do my visiting teaching first."

1

- "I feel guilty anytime I leave my kids in order to do something for myself."
- "My Relief Society lessons aren't nearly as good as Sister Perfection's. I'd better put in some more hours working on those handouts and gift baskets."
- "I didn't send out a Christmas letter last year; I'd better do a spring letter immediately. I don't know—does that sound dumb?"
- "This diet is not working. Oh, let's face it. I'm so out of control. I'll never get this body back into shape."

Do you feel stressed, overworked, resentful, frustrated, or any of those other lovely draining adjectives that seem to define womanhood?

I hit my max at one point when I had four little boys—ages 9, 4, 2, and a newborn—and a new Dalmatian puppy. I felt like I had a shackle on each limb plus a neck chain! I think the best word to describe my state of being was "confined." Let me share two entries from my journal.

April 23

This week has been a bit of a trial. Just for Parker's future information, he is being a Terrible Two right now. This week alone he got red lipstick all over the bathroom carpet, wrote with red chalk *and* rolled a red jawbreaker (wet, of course) all over his carpet, wrote with colored chalk all over the walls, put toothpaste all over his dresser, spilled three bowls of cereal everywhere in the house, and for his finale, got a new bag of cookies, dumped them on the tile, STOMPED on them, and then walked (yes, with chocolate all over his shoes) through the living room to eat the remaining whole cookies under the dining room table! That's in one week!! He is lucky he survived!!

Oh, yeah, he also got in my car and jammed a ton of quarters into the cassette tape deck and then crammed in the tape. It is now broken. All I have to say is this, "YOU OWE ME KID!! IN A MAJOR WAY!!"

Sunday, July 7, 1991

Well, another terrible week. Man, this journal is depressing. I sure chose a lousy time to write one. My poor kids are going to get a complex when they read this later. Maybe they will realize what a lot of work it was and will appreciate all the sacrifice. Doubtful. Poor Connor is going to get a complex—he asks me every day, "Why are you crying, Mom?" I just say I'm having a bad day.

How can I explain that I feel like a tiger in a cage, pacing back and forth, back and forth. How can I explain that I have chosen to stay home with my children so that they aren't raised by strangers, but that this decision is DRIVING ME NUTS? How do I explain that we're always broke because I'm not working, and that I want to work but I can't because I have chosen to stay home with the kids and that while I believe that is a good choice, it is a really difficult one. Oh, well. Life isn't always fun.

It was at this point that my husband suggested that maybe I take some time for myself and go play. That seemed like a good idea. But I literally could not think of what I wanted to do! It was like my play button had been disconnected for so long that I couldn't even come up with *one* thing that sounded fun or appealing.

I began calling other women to see if they wanted to do something. And one after another declined. "Oh, I'm sorry, but I've got a big week at work this week." "I'm just really busy with the kids." "I have too much on my plate right now." Not one would take the time to go have fun!

I decided playtime was something I would have to do for myself. So I began to ponder: What did *I* want to do?

Now I figure that many of us are in this position. So let's do a little experiment.

Close your eyes and remember what you were like when you were sixteen. What did you like to do? How did you dress? Did you do sports or physical activities? What was fun for you when you were sixteen? Okay, open your eyes. (I know, how could you be reading this if they were closed? Work with me here!)

3

Now a simple question: Why aren't you doing that stuff now? And more broadly, "Why don't women play?"

The answer is quite clear: Women feel *guilty*. We feel guilty about all the things we *should* be doing.

- I can't go on a date with my husband because I *should* spend more quality time with our children.
- I can't go out with girlfriends because I *should* visit my elderly grandmother instead.
- I can't take up a hobby because I *should* do my family history work.
- I can't exercise because I *should* clean the house.

We let guilt paralyze us.

I know a woman who hasn't read a book in decades because every time she feels the desire, she thinks, "Well, I really *should* read my scriptures instead."

We women feel guilt over every mistake we've made, every shortcoming we have, and every good thing that we're not presently doing because we haven't been able to cram it into our overflowing schedule yet!

It's interesting to compare this to men. Men feel they *deserve* time off. They've worked hard. They've taken care of their families and their responsibilities and now they're allowed to take it easy and have some fun. Women typically don't think this way. We not only don't feel we deserve time off but when we *do* take time off, we feel guilty about it!

The "Perfect Woman"

Part of the reason women feel this guilt so keenly is clearly the fault of the "Perfect Woman." You know who she is. She's out there—and she's perfect.

If I were to ask you to describe the Perfect Woman, you'd have quick answers:

Clearly, she is a size six. No question about that. She has been married a long time to a really important man. He's the stake president. And she's the stake Relief Society president. And they have eight kids—four boys and four girls—evenly spaced. And she homeschools them all. Yeah, and they all play musical instruments—beautifully. And she's a, a, . . . a *neurosurgeon,* and she works out of her home, only part-time.

She has her family history done back to the Dark Ages (and is praying for help to find the rest). She sews matching clothes for the whole family. She has a huge garden and cans most of their food. She makes a loaf of whole-wheat bread from her food storage every day. Her scriptures are completely marked and color-coded, and she studies them for an hour every morning and every night. She is taking a class in Mandarin in order to be able to serve a mission.

Her house is beautifully decorated and always immaculate. Her hair and nails are perfectly done. Her clothes are beautiful. She feeds the homeless every week, and she has created a foundation to help the entire country of Bolivia. She is making a quilt with 100 blocks for her grandmother, who is 100. And yes, all the corners of the quilt blocks match perfectly.

Shall we go on?

It sounds ridiculous, doesn't it? And yet, somehow, we all believe that the Perfect Woman exists somewhere.

Now to be honest, those of you who don't know me may not realize that this description is very close to describing me. I was a size six when I was, well, twelve years old. I am married and have been for a long time, but my husband is not the stake president. He's a Scouter. Okay, so to most people that's not a hugely impressive job, but it is to me. While I don't have eight kids, I have thought about homeschooling, but decided that I wanted my sons to survive to adulthood.

I haven't done my family history, but I do think about it often. Is that close? I rarely sew anymore, but I do have a sewing machine. I also have a good supply of wheat, which I dust off regularly. I eat a lot of canned food. I try to study at least a verse a day in my scriptures.

My hair and nails are perfect for brief moments throughout the year, until I get in the car and mess them up. My clothes are functional. Also, I tried once to make a little quilt in Relief Society that only had nine corners but none of them matched. I sewed buttons over the corners instead. It looked pretty cute.

So except for a few hundred minor faults, I'm very near to perfection myself.

My friend Vickie Gunther wrote a poem that describes the Perfect Woman well.

The Girl in a Whirl
by "Dr. Sue" (a.k.a. Vickie Gunther)

Look at me, look at me, look at me now!
You could do what I do if you only knew how.
I study the scriptures one hour each day.
I bake and I garden. I scrub and I pray.

I always keep all the commandments completely.
I speak to my little ones gently and sweetly.
I help in their classrooms! I sew all they wear!
I drive them to practice! I cut all their hair!

I memorize talks by the General Authorities.
I focus on things to be done by priorities.
I keep our home organized, clean and attractive.
I drop by with goodies and see the less-active.

I play the piano! I bless with my talents!
My toilets all sparkle! My checkbooks all balance!
Each week every child gets a one-on-one date.
I attend all my meetings (On time! Never late!)

I'm taking a class on the teachings of Paul,
But that is not all! Oh, no. That is not all . . .

I track my bad habits 'til each is abolished.
I floss everyday! And my toenails are polished!

Our family home evenings are always delightful.
The lessons I give are both fun and insightful.

I do genealogy faithfully, too.
It's easy to do all the things that I do!
I rise each day early, refreshed and awake.
I know all the names of each youth in my stake!

I read to my children! I help all my neighbors!
I bless the community, too, with my labors.
I write in my journal! I sing in the choir!
Each day, I write "thank you's" to those I admire.

I exercise and I cook menus gourmet.
My visiting teaching is done the first day!
(I also go do it for someone who missed hers.
I love filling in for my cherished ward sisters.)

I chart resolutions and check off each goal.
I seek each "lost lamb" on my Primary roll.
I bottle our produce each summer and fall.
But that is not all! Oh, no. That is not all . . .

I went back to school to update my degree.
My studying earned me a new PhD
I split with the Sisters who cover our ward
To spread the glad truth that the Gospel's restored.

I go to the temple at least once a week.
I make my girls' prom dresses—modest, yet chic.
My sons were all Eagles when they were fourteen!
My kids get straight A's! And their bedrooms are clean!

I have my own business to help earn some money.
I always look beautifully groomed for my honey.
I grind my own wheat and I bake all our bread.
I plan our nutritious meals six months ahead.

I make sure I rotate our two-year's supply.
My shopping for Christmas is done by July!
(It's out of the way early on for a reason.
I then can prepare for the real Christmas season.)

These things are not hard. It's good if you do them.
You can if you try! Just set goals and pursue them!
It's easy to do all the things that I do!
If you plan and work smart, you can do them all too!

"It's easy!" she said . . .
. . . and then,
she dropped dead.[1]

We all laugh about the Perfect Woman, but how many of us secretly compare ourselves constantly to this standard? It's like we carry around a huge backpack filled with rocks and wonder why we're tired! And every now and again, we sit down and pull out a rock to pound ourselves over the head: "I really should be canning my food. My grandma did. I only have six kids under eight. I should just get up at 4 AM and get this done!" On and on we go, heaping on the *guilt!*

The "Celestial Woman"

Let's pause for a moment in our guilt-fest and ask this important question, "What is *required* to enter into the celestial kingdom?"

Do I have to be a size six to qualify? Don't think so.

Will the Lord ask if I had an "important" calling? Definitely not.

But what if I'm not married? Isn't that a deal breaker? Well, no, even the prophets have said it isn't.

Do I need to can, quilt, bake, sew, and organize to get in? Guess not.

So what's left? What *is* required?

Perhaps we can begin with this important goal: We should *want* to *become* a "Celestial Woman." If we have the desire, we will have the motivation to begin to seek out ways to strengthen our spirituality. As we focus on our desire to become a Celestial Woman and to live a more celestial life, we'll naturally increase our desire to have faith, repent, and try to be better every day. Our desire will draw us closer to the temple and to our family. We'll honor the covenants we have already made and strive to keep the commandments we may find challenging. We'll develop charity in our hearts and want to serve others.

The prophet Alma spoke of this as he taught how a powerful faith can grow from the simple righteous *desire* to believe, a *desire* to be better (see Alma 32).

So do we desire to be Celestial Women? Okay, then. Let's do it!

Let's talk about choices for a moment. We can select our own good works. Life is a smorgasbord of good choices. You will not be penalized for picking ham over chicken or cake instead of pie.

The Lord discusses this principle in Doctrine and Covenants 58:26–28.

> For behold, it is not meet that I should command in all things; for he that is compelled in all things, the same is a slothful and not a wise servant; wherefore he receiveth no reward.
>
> Verily I say, men should be anxiously engaged in a good cause, and do many things of their own free will, and bring to pass much righteousness;
>
> For the power is in them, wherein they are agents unto themselves. And inasmuch as men do good they shall in nowise lose their reward.

The Lord will not rap you on the knuckles for your choices in selecting one good work over another. He will bless you for all your good works. He knows you have tons of problems and are doing the best you can. He is interested in your improvement and your progress. He does not condemn you.

We are condemning ourselves, and it is a total waste of time. We beat ourselves up for mistakes and choices that we've made and then we wallow in our guilt.

Elder Dallin H. Oaks discussed this in his talk, "Sins and Mistakes." I remember hearing him at BYU Education Week and finally "getting it" as to where all this guilt should fit in. He said,

> Sins result from willful disobedience of laws we have received by explicit teaching or by the Spirit of Christ that teaches every man the general principles of right and wrong. For sins, the remedy is to chasten and encourage repentance.
>
> Mistakes result from ignorance of the laws of God or of the workings of the universe or of people he has created. For mistakes, the remedy is to correct the mistake, not to condemn the actor. . . .
>
> We should seek to avoid mistakes, since some mistakes have very painful consequences. But we do not seek to avoid mistakes at all costs. . . . To avoid all possibility of error is to avoid all possibility of growth. . . .
>
> . . . Innocent mistakes can be a source of growth and progress.[2]

Guilt, then, is to be saved for sins. In fact, guilt is very important and useful in this respect. It causes us to feel sorrow and to repent from sins that would otherwise prevent our growth. But somehow, we've extended guilt to include all our mistakes and imperfections and every good thing that we're not currently doing!

Dr. Laura Schlessinger is always rapping on women when they call her radio program and say, "I feel guilty . . ." She'll nail them and ask, "Why do you feel guilty for simply making a choice?" Truth is, we don't like to feel bad or uncomfortable and so we use *guilt* as a default word.

So for starters, let's eliminate that word from our vocabulary unless it refers to sin. ("Oh, great," you say. "Now I'll feel guilty just *thinking* the word!" This is only a suggestion. Nothing to feel guilty about!)

Consider for one moment. Do you honestly think an angel is

standing at the pearly gates with a checklist?—"Hmm, let's see. A size eight, well that's acceptable . . . barely. Can you bake bread? No? Well . . . Do you know how to work with gluten? Good. Check! Okay, did you do graduate work in college? Good. Check! Now, did you learn how to quilt? No? Hmmmm. Were you a Relief Society president? Only a nursery leader? Oh, too bad. You know, I just don't think you made it. How about a nice terrestrial kingdom slot?"

Somehow I don't see that happening. And yet we run around our lives acting as if those are the requirements the Lord has asked of us!

It seems that we often use worldly standards to determine whether we are fit for the kingdom. But those worldly standards just don't apply. It's like we spend our whole lives cramming for a test without realizing we're using the wrong study guide!

On top of that we have to deal with the whole competition trap. We compare ourselves incessantly to the Perfect Woman or if not to her, then to "Sister Near-Perfection" who lives in our ward or on our street.

At what point do we realize that we are not in a race! We are not competing! Whether you do something better or worse than someone else doesn't add brownie points to your scorecard nor remove them from hers. We will be discussing competition more in the next chapter.

Our lives can take on a pace and a pressure that drives us faster and faster to do more and more until our lists become endless. As I pondered this thought, I was moved by the insight shared by Barbara Timothy Bowen in *An Emotional First-Aid Kit for Mothers*.

> Actually, it was a change in perspective that altered my plate spinning and made me view everything I did as a mother differently. Perhaps it began when I first read the near-death experience in George Ritchie's book, *Return from Tomorrow*, in which the glorious being of light asks him what he has done with his life. After reviewing his worldly accomplishments—such as having become an Eagle Scout and having been accepted into medical school—he realizes to his horror and amazement that the only

questions he's being asked, the only question he'll ever really be asked is "How much have you *loved* with your life?"

Now, I know this is probably not a new thought for you, and it was not a new thought for me. But when I read it, it hit me as though I were hearing it for the first time, and I cried inside, "How much *have* I loved with my life?" Suddenly my long list of daily demands, my endless plate spinning, seemed only important in accomplishing this one goal, and I began a new way of looking at my role as a mother. . . . Now I had only one main plate to spin, and the voice behind it was asking how much I was loving.[3]

"How Much Have You Loved in Your Life?"

"How much have you *loved* in your life?" What an important question! Suddenly, all my obsession over my omnipresent to-do list seemed to fade away.

I pondered Christ's life. He had no money and appeared to lack worldly success. He did not care one whit for worldly standards. Instead, he filled his life with good works and love. He was continually about his Father's business—the work of saving souls.

Pondering Christ's life can help us plan our own lives and the focus we apply to it.

I'll admit it. I like checklists and making plans and feel I have good organizational skills. Those qualities help me personally to stay on track. But they don't work for everyone. And certainly God views our life and our spiritual development as a process, not a checklist. He does not peruse and review our personal report card. Nor should we hold up our own list: "Let's see. Family home evening? Check. Regular church attendance? Check. Family prayer daily? Check. Individual prayer? Check. Okay, I'm ready for the celestial kingdom!" Yes, these are all important elements of a righteous life, but in the end, the Lord will look not only at what we have *done* but also at who we have *become.*

How have we developed? Have we become more like Christ?

Have we developed charity—that pure love that is not only the Savior's work, but is also at the heart of who he is?

Life is a process to learn charity. To learn *to love*. The *process* of learning to love is important. Whether you learn and experience that process through maintaining your home and trying daily to teach your children to get along with each other, or whether you're a president of a large company and trying to get along with coworkers, the process of learning to love is crucial and tailored to each situation. The importance lies in what you are learning through the process.

The world takes a completely different view. One lifestyle is considered quite unimportant and menial, while another is considered hugely important. We need to keep a *godly* perspective on what our work is here on the earth and not be distracted by the *worldly* perspective.

Each of us can use the experiences of our life to learn to love. We can explore each opportunity to grow. But it is our choice whether we cut our growth and development short by reveling in the worldly success we've achieved, or whether we continue to humbly pursue growth in that important life lesson of love.

Focus on "Becoming"

As I mentioned before, focusing on what you've done is not as important in this learning process as focusing on who you have *become*.

Elder Dallin H. Oaks spoke of this in his great talk, "The Challenge to Become," where he stated:

> The Final Judgment is not just an evaluation of a sum total of good and evil acts—what we have *done*. It is an acknowledgment of the final effect of our acts and thoughts—what we have *become*. It is not enough for anyone just to go through the motions. The commandments, ordinances, and covenants of the gospel are not a list of deposits required to be made in some heavenly account.

13

The gospel of Jesus Christ is a plan that shows us how to become what our Heavenly Father desires us to become. . . .

We are challenged to move through a process of conversion toward that status and condition called eternal life. This is achieved not just by doing what is right, but by doing it for the right reason—for the pure love of Christ. The Apostle Paul illustrated this in his famous teaching about the importance of charity (see 1 Cor. 13). The reason charity never fails and the reason charity is greater than even the most significant acts of goodness he cited is that charity, "the pure love of Christ" (Moro. 7:47), is not an *act* but a *condition* or state of being. Charity is attained through a succession of acts that result in a conversion. Charity is something one becomes. Thus, as Moroni declared, "except men shall *have* charity they cannot inherit" the place prepared for them in the mansions of the Father (Ether 12:34; emphasis added). . . .

Instead of being judgmental about others, we should be concerned about ourselves. We must not give up hope. We must not stop striving. We are children of God, and it is possible for us to become what our Heavenly Father would have us become.[4]

Elder Oaks's words make me think of my friend Izzy. When I was Relief Society president many years ago, Izzy was my counselor. She was old enough to be my mother, and I loved her to pieces. Izzy is elderly now and knows that she is approaching the final years of her life. She has had a long life filled with much heartache. She is divorced and three of her six children have died in tragic circumstances. She does not have much money and lives in a small condo. I know that the world looks at Izzy and doesn't see much that is successful or impressive in her life. But I look at Izzy and I see who she has become. You should have seen her during the week she spent at a nursing home. She was Miss Popular!

She was in pain and recuperating from several falls and many ailments, yet she radiated love and friendship. There was a constant parade through her room of visitors and friends she had gathered over the years through her love and kindness.

But the evenings were especially interesting. I went to visit her one evening and found a group of seniors in wheelchairs around her door and inside her room. I said, "What's going on here?" Izzy and her roommate laughed. "Well, we just have so much fun and laughter that everyone wants to come here in the evenings! We talk and share, and we're having a great time."

I was astounded. My friend was in a nursing home for physical rehab and yet she was sharing love and joy with everyone she came into contact with. I wasn't sure they would let her come home! Izzy has true charity in her heart and that heart expands to include all who come within her circle of love.

Endure to the End

Heavenly Father wants us to have *joy* in our lives. He does *not* want us to be miserable, drudging through the mud of trials, with no hope for happiness. The commandments and the gospel he has given us are like rocks in the river we can step on to return to him. This doesn't mean we're not going to get our feet wet, or that we won't fall in, but we have been given the path and the life preserver of repentance. And through it all, Heavenly Father has assured us that he is with us always.

He asks us to do one thing, "If you keep my commandments and *endure to the end* you shall have eternal life, which gift is the greatest of all the gifts of God" (D&C 14:7; emphasis added).

In other words, "Please hang in there and work on keeping the commandments and you will be blessed for it." It doesn't sound like he wants us to be miserable, as though he said that phrase with teeth clenched—"enduuuure to the end"—instead, it sounds like life should be a joyful pursuit of the greatest gift God can offer us.

The Lord explains his goal for the tenor of our lives in 2 Nephi 2:25: "[wo]men are, that they might have joy." This is what Heavenly Father wants for us. He wants us to have joy! President Gordon B. Hinckley, whom I loved for his sense of humor, said, "In all living have much of fun and laughter. Life is to be enjoyed, not just endured."[5]

Let's face it. Isn't that what we want for our children and our families? Isn't that what we want for ourselves? We want joy—pure and simple. Somehow, it goes beyond being happy or having fun.

Think about that word—joy—for a moment. What do you think of?

I think of my whole family vacationing in Yellowstone Park. Togetherness. *Joy.*

I think of being in a tent, snuggled up in a sleeping bag, listening to the rain. Contentment. *Joy.*

I think of sitting quietly and watching a hummingbird mother feed her babies. Life! *Joy.*

I think of finishing a large project that took effort and growth on my part. Satisfaction. *Joy.*

I think of eating a hot fudge sundae with nuts and whipped cream. Okay, that's *pure* joy!

In our lives, we can experience joy in keeping the commandments, as encouraged by the Lord. We can experience joy in correcting mistakes and moving forward. We can experience joy in selecting our own good works.

It's so important to become a joyful person while we are here on earth. Happiness should not be something we delay, thinking it's only possible after we've left behind all the difficulties we've been gritting our teeth through in this life. In Mormon 9:14 we read: "And then cometh the judgment of the Holy One upon them; and then cometh the time that . . . he that is happy shall be happy still; and he that is unhappy shall be unhappy still." Telling words. If we are to be happy and joyful, it is to happen here and now.

Our lives can be filled with happiness and joy, but the choice is up to us.

Happiness is:

> Courageously doing what you want to do, even if you are scared.
> Experiencing your life as an exciting journey.
> Stimulating your mind and caring for your body.
> *Realizing that you already have everything you need to make yourself happy.*

Knowing that you are the only one who can decide what is right or wrong for you.

Accepting that you are okay even when you blunder and learn from your mistakes.

Knowing that what people say or do is a reflection of *them* not you.

Listening to your inner wisdom.

Giving and receiving love unconditionally.

—Anonymous[6]

We can choose to be happy and to have a joyful life *right now*, but too many of us have let the joy in our lives be snuffed out because we are concentrating too much on the perfection list. I love President Hinckley's constant reminders that we need to have some fun, "A little play and a little loafing are good."[7]

Catch the Joy!

So let's let the list go. Let's throw off our guilt like an old coat that doesn't fit anymore and bring more fun, laughter, and joy into our lives. Let's catch some joy!

We each find joy and happiness in a different way. So what is it for you? Where do you find joy?

If you're like me, it may take a while to get in touch with those joyful feelings again. That's okay. Let's take that time to develop our own "Personal Play Plan." What do you want to do? What would be on your list?

I began asking myself those questions and writing them down, a few here and a few there. Over the years I've asked many women what would be on their list and have had many wonderful responses:

Go sky diving! (The woman was about to turn 70!)
Go to the family history library once a week (My dear friend
	Libby has cleared her schedule to do this, and she loves it.
	As I mentioned, we're all different.)
Take archaeology classes

More playtime with my children
Learn to play the piano (by a woman in her 80s)
Go scuba diving
Rollerblade with my dog
Meditate
Go to the temple weekly
Learn to quilt
Try woodworking
Take a nap (my personal favorite)
Read the entire Book of Mormon
Take a cruise
Take up oil painting
Write my mom's personal history
Date my husband weekly
Write a book
Learn to tap dance
Get involved in my political party
Play my violin again
Grow a garden
Take a yoga class
Take a walk in the morning
Call my mother every week, just to chat
Travel

The list could go on and on. I have found that the answers to the question of what brings you joy are unique to each woman. No two are alike. I've also noticed what happens to a woman's face when she talks about these things—her eyes light up, a small smile begins, and she glows as she talks about the wonderful, fun, interesting, or new things she could do with her life.

Personal Play Plan in Action

So, like a little whipped cream on top of a sundae, let's talk about how we can put our Personal Play Plan into action!

First, write down what you like to do or what you *would* like to do. If your life is like mine, it's hard to remember things in the swirl of living. So start your list now! And let it grow year after year after year!

Second, start small, but do start. You may not be able to go scuba diving immediately, but you could take a mask and snorkel to the ocean and try it out. You may not be able to write an entire book right now, but you could write a short essay or start a blog. The important thing is to start. Start this week. Pick some small part you can do now and do it! Trust that over time your talent—and your joy—will grow.

I wanted to try painting, so I started small by taking a class to learn tole painting, which I'd always admired. I had a ball. I wasn't very good, but I had so much fun!

Third, own your joy. I promise you that you will probably encounter resistance. One thing that brings me pure joy is taking a nap. Currently I have five part-time jobs, four kids, three volunteer positions, two church callings, and a husband to care for. My days are often exhausting! So I take a nap whenever I can.

One day I was sleeping and my son answered the phone. It was the lady from the insurance company. I returned her call later in the day. I will always remember her snide and snippy voice. "Well," she said in a huff, "I hope you enjoyed your *nap!*" I laughed, "Yes, I did! And I'm hoping to take one again tomorrow." She was not amused . . . but I sure was!

It seems like people—especially women—don't like it when you rock the boat. If you're going around with a giddy smile on your face, they're going to be jealous. If you're talking about some wonderful thing you're doing, they may not want to hear it. That's okay. Own your joy anyway!

We may have to be relentless in our pursuit to bring play back into our lives. Yes, to everything there is a time and a season but *no* season should be pure drudgery. We may have to adjust our pursuit of joy to fit our seasons, but we should never eliminate it entirely. And we will have different types of play because we are all different. Never let someone else's reaction interrupt your pursuit of your joy.

And finally, cut yourself some slack! This Personal Play Plan is not another "Perfection To-Do List" to flog yourself with. This is a suggestion for a way that might help you catch the joy in your life.

I remember running into a woman a year after I had spoken on this subject.

"Well, I haven't gone on my cruise yet. I guess I've failed," she said. (Here was a woman who had missed the trees of joy in the forest of guilt.)

I stopped her right there. "Have you thought about it this past year?"

She smiled and her face lit up. "Yes, I have thought about it. And I've been talking to other people about it. I haven't decided where to go yet, but I've been saving my money. I've been studying about Germany, and I'm thinking about maybe doing one of those river cruises." For her, even planning the fun had become fun in and of itself.

There is something wonderful that will happen when you begin to catch the joy again in your life. A ripple effect will grow. You'll have more to talk about with others.

I was visiting an office recently and one young woman told me all about her upcoming humanitarian trip to Mexico and the charity she was working with. Another middle-aged woman related to me the story of her latest scuba diving trip. (I was so surprised to hear that she loved to dive!) Another woman talked about a book she was writing. And yet another woman shared with me all the things she was doing with her grandchildren. What a wonderful experience! I was so energized just by talking to all of these women who were actively pursuing fun in a variety of ways.

Imagine the end of your day as you're sitting with your roommates over dinner or with your husband and kids. "Guess what I learned about today? I studied the white rhinoceros in Zambia. It is fascinating! And I was able to rollerblade around the entire block with the dog without falling down once!" You will be quite an interesting person!

Another result of making time to play will be that you will have more energy in your tanks to serve others and do all those necessary things in your life. We have so many things that we must do, so many plates to keep spinning. But if we never stop to catch some joy, the guilt will burn us up.

I'm constantly explaining this concept to mothers of young children. Having some personal time is extremely difficult, and many moms say they feel guilty just taking those brief times away from their children. I ask them to stop and think about how they feel after their break. Most moms feel energized and ready to go back and tackle the real world.

This is also true of women who are working full-time. It can be so hard to take time off to find some personal joy. And yet, when they do, they find they have much more stamina to return to their work duties.

Finally, when we make the effort to fill our lives with more joy, we find that we are filled with greater charity. We will notice others more and have the energy and interest to reach out and help them. Guilt is a very selfish endeavor, and when we are swept up in feeling that way often, it's like we have blinders on. When we can toss the guilt aside, we can find the joy that comes when we help others and are aware of their needs and concerns.

I listen to a local radio show hosted by Jeff and Jer. Every day they sign off the same way, "This is the two and only, Jeff and Jer! This has been the best day of our lives! See ya!" I'm always intrigued by that. I think, "How can they say that? What if something bad is happening? And what about me? Is this the best day of my life?"

And each time I ponder that question, I realize the answer can be yes. Each day that we toss the guilt aside and catch the joy can be the best day of our lives. Each day can have moments of joy— breathtaking moments, quiet moments, invigorating moments, sweet moments of joy. And that is worth the effort.

CHAPTER 2

Women of Being, Not Comparison

L et's enjoy a short story.

Once upon a time, there was a little girl named Goldilocks. She went for a walk in the forest. Pretty soon, she came upon a house. She knocked and, when no one answered, she walked right in.

At the table in the kitchen, there were three bowls of porridge. Goldilocks was hungry. She tasted the porridge from the first bowl.

"This porridge is too hot!" she exclaimed.

So, she tasted the porridge from the second bowl.

"This porridge is too cold," she said.

So, she tasted the last bowl of porridge.

"Ahhh, this porridge is just right," she said happily, and she ate it all up.

After she'd eaten the three bears' breakfasts she decided she was feeling a little tired. So, she walked into the living room where she saw three chairs. Goldilocks sat in the first chair to rest her feet.

"This chair is too big!" she exclaimed.

So she sat in the second chair.

"This chair is too big, too!" she whined.

So she tried the last and smallest chair.

"Ahhh, this chair is just right," she sighed. But just as she settled down into the chair to rest, it broke into pieces!

Goldilocks was very tired by this time, so she went upstairs to the bedroom. She lay down in the first bed, but it was too hard. Then she lay in the second bed, but it was too soft. Then she lay down in the third bed and it was just right. Goldilocks fell asleep.[1]

And yada yada yada, she encounters the bears and end of story.

Now many of us may look at Goldilocks and think, "Man, is she ever picky!" Others may say, "No, Goldi just knows what she wants and goes after it. She is discerning." And still others may say, "Let's first discuss the whole breaking-and-entering issue, shall we?"

The story of Goldilocks and the Three Bears is the classic story of comparison. As Goldilocks compared her alternatives, only one was suitable for her particular tastes.

Women excel in comparison. Many of us have this down to a fine art. Within seconds of meeting a woman, we have compared her to ourselves and to every woman we have ever met and have assigned her a score based on those comparisons. It is amusing, but so true.

If you met my friend Sue, would you think she's too tall? Too short? Too skinny? Too fat? Sue is Sue, and she is just right. If you met my sister, Andrea, would you think she is too smart or too dumb? Too quiet or too loud? Andrea is Andrea, and she is just right. (To be honest, she's not at all quiet, but I happen to like that about her.)

I could introduce you to my friend Edah who lives in Zambia. By American standards, Edah is fat, lower-middle-class, and loud. By African standards, Edah is beautiful, rich, and delightful. What is she by God's standards? Just right.

Comparing

Now we must admit, it's human nature to compare. It's how we make choices in life. We compare apples to oranges. We debate our favorite flavor of pie. We compare colors to select our favorite carpeting. We compare music to select a CD to listen to. Comparison is a necessary process in life.

It's also human nature to compare people to each other and to ourselves. It's how we understand one another and how we understand ourselves.

But do we ever really know the *truth* of others' lives? A person may have unseen burdens that we know nothing about. I could show you a picture of a group of women and tell you that one woman has multiple sclerosis, one is going through a nasty divorce, one is caring for her elderly mom and paying all the expenses, and one has struggled with dyslexia her whole life—and you would have no idea which person was dealing with which problem. They simply look like normal, everyday women. You cannot see their burdens so the comparison is *always* faulty.

Have you ever had an experience when you realized you might be judging someone unfairly? I once met a young mom who was absolutely beautiful and who had a lovely home. I had assumed she was your average, sweet Mormon mom. But as time went on, her behavior didn't match that picture. I could not figure it out. I kept thinking, "What is *wrong* with her? Why can't she handle this or that?"

After I had known her for several years, we went out to lunch and she began to tell me her story. I sat dumbfounded as she related how horrendous her childhood had been and the terrible things she had suffered. I looked at her in amazement, realizing that if those things had happened to me, I would likely have been curled up in the corner, unable to function. I was immediately filled with love and understanding for her. I felt so badly for all the assumptions and comparisons I had made. I was so proud of her for carrying on despite the high degree of difficulty in her life. And now when I encounter people who wonder "What is wrong with her?" I am her biggest champion.

Another time I met a woman who was very unique. Her husband did all the cooking (which I happen to think is heaven on earth) and her house was filled with all kinds of animals. She had a kind of Bohemian outlook and behavior. She certainly wasn't your cookie-cutter Mormon woman. I always thought, "My, my, she's certainly *different.*" (And not always in a positive way!)

Then one day, she told me her story. Her mom had been married five times, and her dad ran a bar. Her siblings all had significant struggles, and her home life had been really . . . different! It explained so much. Now I am so impressed with her constant and total devotion to the gospel. I understand her ability to get along with all kinds of people, and her propensity to take in lost puppies . . . and lost souls and lost relatives. She is an incredibly loving and open woman. And wonderfully different.

Comparisons have been made about me as well that were way off base. I'll share two examples. I was married, the mother of a young son, and finishing up law school. My husband and I had been trying to get pregnant with our second child for years. I had suffered a miscarriage already and we were undergoing infertility treatments at the same time as I was studying for the bar exam (no stress there).

Having heard that I was done with law school, a man in my ward came up to me and in a most unkind and judgmental voice said, "Well, I hope now you will settle down and have more children!" I looked at him stunned. Luckily, I had developed quite a backbone by then. I looked him clearly in the eye and said, "My husband and I have lost a child and have been in infertility treatments for a year. Before you judge someone next time, perhaps you will get the facts first." He sputtered with bugged eyes and then fled.

The second example is not quite as dramatic. My family had recently moved and I was practicing law part-time from my home, but I didn't talk about that part of my life very much. One day, I was in a T-shirt and jeans, visiting my new friend, Izzy. She said to me, "I heard the funniest rumor in the ward. Somebody said you were a lawyer!" When I told her I was, she looked shocked and said,

"Well, you certainly don't look like one or act like one!" We both laughed, and I took that as a great compliment.

We truly have no idea what goes on in people's lives. Any comparison we make to them is based on our *perception* of who they are and often our perception is way off base. Experiences they have had in the past, current pain and problems that no one knows about, disabilities or conditions they may have—those can all change the picture completely.

On the other hand, someone's opportunities or advantages may not be known either. We could look at the same group photo of women and we would not know that one has a genius-level IQ, another has an amazing job because her dad is golfing buddies with the president of a company, another has a photographic memory, and another one went to a top-notch school with the president's daughter, and on and on we go.

In all our comparisons, we often cannot see another's gifts, skills, or opportunities. We have no idea what comes easily to them or what doors were opened for them that perhaps were not available to us. So we compare ourselves negatively, not realizing what is behind the scenes.

When we compare, we can compare only to façades, to what we see and perceive. Even if we think we know someone well, there is always a deeper part that is hidden from us. I've known my mom for fifty years, and yet there are still things about her I do not know. My husband has known me for twenty-eight years, and he'll tell you there are many things about me he still doesn't know. (I'm saving them up to spread them out over the decades. Keeps him on his toes.)

So the problem with comparing is that it is never fair, it is never equal, and it is always, always apples to oranges.

Sheri Dew discussed this problem at length:

> [Joseph Smith] said that "it is natural for females to have feelings of charity" (*History of the Church*, 4:605).
> Knowing this, Lucifer works hard at undermining our divine gift. All too often we fall into traps he has designed that estrange

us from each other. He delights when we gossip and criticize and judge, when we stew over perceived offenses or measure ourselves against each other, or when we succumb to such envy that we even begrudge each other's successes. . . .

How often have all of us made judgments that are equally unfair? Why can't we resist the urge to second-guess and evaluate each other? Why do we judge everything from the way we keep house to how many children we do or do not have? Sometimes I wonder if the final judgment will be a breeze compared with what we've put each other through here on earth![2]

It is strange to think that probably every one of us has been judged and compared unfairly, and yet we still continue to do it to ourselves and others.

We drive to church and notice that the Hansens have gotten a new van, and we feel badly about our old van. We notice that Shelly has a great new dress on and seems to have lost weight, and we are smitten with guilt that our diet is failing rapidly. We hear a talk from little Sammie who is absolutely the most perfect child, and wonder if our daughter will ever learn to speak with respect, much less intelligence. In Sunday School we listen to the most amazing lesson from Brother Sanchez, and we remember how we painfully struggle to teach a basic lesson. Then off to Relief Society we go, where the incredible presidency sits before us—two lawyers, one small-business owner, and one beautiful mom whose husband is the life of the party—and we feel so inadequate.

What we don't realize is that the Hansen's old van was totaled and the insurance payout was lousy. We don't know that Shelly has lost weight because her father recently passed away and the new dress was for his funeral. We don't realize that Sammie had a brain tumor when he was young and is wise beyond his years because of his unique trials. And Brother Sanchez's father taught religion at BYU and gave his son his amazing files on the course subject. And we have no idea that the Relief Society president is struggling with her son; one counselor is trying to cope after her mother's recent, massive stroke, heart surgery, and surgery for melanoma; another counselor is struggling with deafness; and the beautiful mom has had a tumultuous past surviving an abusive first marriage.

And we walk out of church feeling bad about ourselves. How ridiculous is that? And yet we do this to ourselves week after week. It's time to wake up and stop the cycle.

Comparison is the foundation of a giant, unnecessary "guilt-fest." We pile on guilt after guilt after guilt as we compare ourselves to others and find ourselves lacking. The simple sentence "I'm not as [insert adjective here] as [insert name here]" generates huge amounts of guilt. "I'm not as slim as Mary" and we feel guilty about our lack of self-control. "I'm not as smart as Joann" and we feel guilty we didn't finish college. "I'm not as patient as Elena" and we feel guilty about our parenting skills. Comparison feeds our guilt like fuel to a fire.

The reverse can also happen. We sit in a PTA meeting and feel smug that we are a righteous Mormon mom and that our family never struggles with drugs or pornography or anything else they're discussing in the meetings. And we are dead wrong.

Merrill Christensen spoke of the truth behind comparisons in a devotional at BYU:

> If we are content to simply be better than the world, comparing ourselves to its standards and practices instead of to the Lord's, we may pride ourselves on the widening gap between us and the world. . . . At the same time [we are] dangerously oblivious to the increasing distance between us and the standards of righteousness we have covenanted to keep. . . .
>
> . . . Your value to Him is independent of your body mass index; your accomplishments in arts, academics or athletics; your possessions, popularity, or marital status; your current calling in the Church; or any other thing that can be a source of comparison and competition.[3]

I love that. Our true value, our divine worth, is independent of any of the mortal trappings that surround us.

The truth is only Heavenly Father and Jesus Christ can make righteous comparisons because only they know the *truth* about each of us. They know our individual gifts and abilities. They know our secret desires and the hopes of our heart. They know the pain and degree of difficulty we've experienced on our life's journey. And they know exactly who we have been for an eternity and who we are now. They alone possess this truth about us. They actually know us better than we know ourselves.

The Savior talks about the fairness of this perception in the parable of the servants and the vineyard:

> For the kingdom of heaven is like unto a man that is an householder, which went out early in the morning to hire labourers into his vineyard.
>
> And when he had agreed with the labourers for a penny a day, he sent them into his vineyard.
>
> And he went out about the third hour, and saw others standing idle in the marketplace,
>
> And said unto them; Go ye also into the vineyard, and whatsoever is right I will give you. And they went their way.
>
> Again he went out about the sixth and ninth hour, and did likewise.
>
> And about the eleventh hour he went out, and found others standing idle, and saith unto them, Why stand ye here all the day idle?
>
> They say unto him, Because no man hath hired us. He saith unto them, Go ye also into the vineyard; and whatsoever is right, that shall ye receive.
>
> So when even was come, the lord of the vineyard saith unto his steward, Call the labourers, and give them their hire, beginning from the last unto the first.
>
> And when they came that were hired about the eleventh hour, they received every man a penny.
>
> But when the first came, they supposed that they should have received more; and they likewise received every man a penny.

> And when they had received it, they murmured against the goodman of the house,
>
> Saying, These last have wrought but one hour, and thou hast made them equal unto us, which have borne the burden and heat of the day.
>
> But he answered one of them, and said, Friend, I do thee no wrong: didst not thou agree with me for a penny?
>
> Take that thine is, and go thy way: I will give unto this last, even as unto thee. (Matthew 20:1–14)

Heavenly Father has provided a plan for each of us to receive eternal life. He knows what each of us has experienced. We're the ones who whine and complain that Sister So-and-So has such an easy life and Brother Thus-and-Such is so perfect. And the Lord reassures us that he knows and he will pass fair and merciful judgment.

One sister thinks, *But I was the Relief Society president! And look, I can still wear my clothes from high school. And I had a year's supply and held amazing family home evenings every single week.* But in her heart she was constantly critical of others.

Another sister thinks, *I struggled every day with chronic pain from fibromyalgia. My marriage is hanging by a thread. And I am so worried about my oldest daughter.* In her heart, though, she was constantly merciful and forgiving.

How shall the Lord reward them? Fairly!

Comparison has another element that is particularly dangerous. Pride. President Ezra Taft Benson spoke of this in his talk, "Beware of Pride."

> Another major portion of this very prevalent sin of pride is enmity toward our fellowmen. We are tempted daily to elevate ourselves above others and diminish them. . . .
>
> The proud make every man their adversary by pitting their intellects, opinions, works, wealth, talents, or any other worldly measuring device against others. In the words of C. S. Lewis: "Pride gets no pleasure out of having something, only out of having more of it than the next man. . . . It is the comparison that

makes you proud: the pleasure of being above the rest. Once the element of competition has gone, pride has gone." (*Mere Christianity* [New York: Macmillan, 1952], 109–10.) . . .

The proud stand more in fear of men's judgment than of God's judgment. . . . "What will men think of me?" weighs heavier than "What will God think of me?" . . .

Pride is a sin that can readily be seen in others but is rarely admitted in ourselves. Most of us consider pride to be a sin of those on the top, such as the rich and the learned, looking down at the rest of us. . . . There is, however, a far more common ailment among us—and that is pride from the bottom looking up. It is manifest in so many ways, such as faultfinding, gossiping, backbiting, murmuring, living beyond our means, envying, coveting, withholding gratitude and praise that might lift another, and being unforgiving and jealous.[4]

I remember hearing this talk and being so surprised by his identification of pride as including those who are criticizing others from the bottom of the pile. It is that comparison mentality, again, which is dangerous.

In the Doctrine and Covenants, the Lord chastised several brethren for these faults:

And let him repent of his sins, for he seeketh the praise of the world. . . .

And also he hath need to repent, for I, the Lord, am not well pleased with him, for he seeketh to excel, and he is not sufficiently meek before me.

Behold, he who has repented of his sins, the same is forgiven, and I, the Lord, remember them no more.

By this ye may know if a man repenteth of his sins—behold, he will confess them and forsake them. (D&C 58:39–43)

Again, it is the habit of comparison that the Lord deplores here. He wants us to understand that it is ridiculous to seek the praise of the world. Not only does the world look only on the surface, but the world's standards are in large part wrong and misguided. He also wants us to understand that when we seek to excel—when we seek to be better than others (as we perceive them)—we are not using correct standards either.

Throughout the scriptures, the Savior reminds us not to rely on the arm of the flesh or to regard the judgments of men. He consistently reminds us that it is only the judgment of God that should concern us. He raises the standard by his example and encourages us to follow him.

Conforming

Another dangerous result of comparison is conforming.

Anna Moses, the world-famous artist known as "Grandma Moses," drew and painted as a child. But then her father told her to put away her silly pastime and focus on working. He struggled as a farmer and probably needed his daughter to help. Anna worked as farmhand for fourteen years, from the age of twelve until she married at age twenty-seven. She didn't take up painting again until she was seventy-four years old in order to help supplement her income. She completed 2,000 works of art and painted until she died at 101.

Her story is often touted as an example of "You're never too old" and it is truly that. But it is also a heartbreaking story of conformance. What if Anna had been encouraged in her art and been able to pursue her talent from her youth onward? Can you imagine the thousands and thousands of works she could have completed? Can you imagine how many other artists she could have influenced? It is heartbreaking to consider that more than sixty years of art were lost because Anna conformed to the influences of her parents and her community and worked hard on the farm. No wonder she painted so much in her advanced years—she was making up for lost time!

Another great artist, Minerva Kohlhepp Teichert, was only four years old when her mother gave her a set of watercolors and encouraged her daughter to paint. With this encouragement, Minerva considered herself an artist from then on.

Everywhere she went, Minerva carried a sketchpad and charcoal or pencil. . . .

By age nineteen, she had scraped together enough money to go to Chicago, where she studied at the Chicago Art Institute under the great draftsman John Vanderpoel, a master of the academic school of painting. Several times during her three-year course she had to go home to earn more money in the fields or in the classroom. But always she returned to follow her dream. . . .

Minerva Teichert spent the rest of her life and her enormous vitality answering these two callings—one to love and serve her family, the other to tell the story of her people and her faith through her art.[5]

Minerva produced over a thousand works of art, many of which can be seen in temples and at Brigham Young University. For a woman who lived on a ranch in Idaho, she left an amazing legacy of art because she stayed true to her unique gifts.

I shall never forget a Relief Society lesson I sat in many years ago. The teacher related that when she had been young, she had been a very gifted musician. I was shocked because I had never, ever seen her do anything musical. She said that she had played viola in the Utah Symphony at a very young age and had played for years. She continued, "And then I met my husband and got married. I decided that it was time in my life to be a wife and a mother and so I sold my viola and have never played again." She said this with pride in her voice, and I wept inside.

Can you imagine the loss? Her children never heard her music. Her friends never heard her music. The world never again heard her music. And to this day, many years later, her music is still lost. All because she felt she should conform to some unwritten notion that "good mothers don't play violas." It makes me sad to this day just thinking about it.

We hear repeatedly that we are to be a peculiar people. I always add the footnote that some are more peculiar than others! And that's great! When we conform, we sometimes give up the unique gifts we have been blessed with and sacrifice our individual mission. So much is lost when we turn from these blessed, individual paths because we think we need to be like everyone else.

How Do We Conform?

We conform in our actions. Think about these familiar situations. The teacher asks, "Do I have a volunteer for the closing prayer?" What happens? Everyone begins studying their shoes in earnest. Or a question is posed in a class and we sit there silent instead of responding. Or we may be with a group of women who are gossiping or husband-bashing and we join in because we don't want to be different. Why do we do this?

We also conform in our attitudes. We may find ourselves accepting worldly beliefs such as "Stay-at-home mothers are wasting their lives," or cultural perceptions like "She's not married so she really doesn't fit in with us." When we stop and truly think about how often we've been swept up in these kinds of ideas, we can see how easily our attitudes have conformed without much thought.

We conform in our dress and appearance. "Well, it's so *hard* to find modest clothing," we say. I doubt that excuse will fly for the Lord. And to keep up with ever-changing fashion trends, we end up wearing clothes that are too tight, too revealing, or even unflattering.

We conform even down to the level of what we own. My dear friends, the Ya-Yas, chuckle over this "obsession with possession" a lot. One of us, Diane, loves to shop, and she knows all the latest fashions. Luckily Diane's husband is very successful, so on occasion she'll trot out her latest purse and gush, "It's a Costaloto!" The rest of us Ya-Yas just look at each other and invariably one of us will say, "Is that a good thing?" Honestly, we couldn't care less about Diane's *purse*. We care about *Diane*.

Finally, there is a type of conformity that is more difficult to identify and combat: self-perception. Sometimes we think, "I'm just [fill in the blank—a woman, a single woman, a mom, a Mormon woman]." Somehow, those labels come with a pre-set identity full of all kinds of limiting or negative connotations that we just accept without challenge.

A great experiment is to play a word-association game with yourself. Say the word "Woman" and what words come to mind? The words that come spontaneously can be very telling. Do you think, "Sweet, weak, protected, nice" or do you think, "Strong, capable, diverse, loving, influential"? Or something in between? Examine all the labels you apply to yourself and the ones the world applies to you. What do these words mean to you? How do you perceive yourself?

When we were teenagers, it seemed like the need to conform was at full tilt. I always found it amusing when my son would say, "I just want to be myself!" and then spend every hour of his waking day desperately trying to be exactly like everybody else at school. Same clothes, same language, same hair, same attitude.

But for some of us, we have a tough time letting go of that overwhelming need to conform and have carried a great deal of it with us into adulthood. For many of us, it may take us into our forties or beyond to begin to let go of that pull of what other people think. How sad that it takes many of us over twenty years to let go of this mind-set!

Now, we *should* conform to gospel principles and commandments. Some might argue that these are limiting and confining. However, the truth is that being obedient to the Lord's commandments will actually help us along in recognizing and achieving our uniqueness. As we have faith in our Savior, we can come to rely on him. As we follow him, we can let go of the grasp of the world. As we develop the gift of the Holy Ghost, we can respond to promptings that come to us, which will help us accomplish our unique mission on earth. Obedience to the gospel frees us in so many ways!

But we *should not* conform to the expectations of the world if they hinder our development, sidetrack us from our mission, or are in conflict with the Lord's commandments. Satan works overtime, layering on fashions and attitudes and norms to influence us in subtle ways. He would have us conform to the world bit by bit. He tries very hard to lead us off our unique path as we strive to live a life of righteousness. How successful is he in your life? Each of us should examine ourselves and our lives in order to honestly answer that question.

Competing

Another aspect of comparison is competing. Just to have a little fun at this point, let's have a little competition. All of you reading this book right now, look at your clothes. If you are wearing two or more items that are white, you win! Congratulations! That was so fun. Let's do it again!

Okay, now count how many "e"s you have in your name. Two? Three? Anybody have five? Alright, you win! Yeah!

Let's do another. How many times in the last week did you eat ice cream? Count it up. Oh, Ethel in Minneapolis just told me she ate ice cream ten times last week so she wins. Sorry, everyone else—you lose.

Now for all the losers out there, how do you feel about the winners? Do you wish you had been a winner?

At this point, you're probably thinking, "Merrilee, this is really stupid! Why do I care who's wearing white today?"

Precisely my point. Who cares?

We are competitive little beasties sometimes, and it can make us all rather crazy. Let me tell you, I'm rather gifted in this area. I feel that competitive little devil rise up in me more often than I'd like. Let me share a story I wrote on confronting this situation.

My Seventh-Grade Science Teacher: Doing Your Best

When I was younger, schoolwork came very easily to me. I was one of those students who had to do very little work to get an A. (Too bad that making dinner every day now isn't as easy for me as taking a test was back then!)

I was in seventh grade in Miller Junior High School. (Can I

just say how much I *hated* junior high? When you're 5'8'' with a pancake chest and thick glasses, every day is sheer torture.) And, of course, I was getting straight As in class and straight Os (for Outstanding) in my citizenship grades.

Frankly, I knew I was smart. I knew all the answers. I could talk circles around any student. And I was still young enough that, most of the time, I didn't hide that fact, which did not help my social standing one bit. I was completely socially inept. Go figure.

It was the first semester, and I got my report card. I was so very cocky as I whipped that thing open—expecting my stellar record to carry on.

And there it was.

Instead of my anticipated "O," I had received an "S" (for "Satisfactory") in citizenship in science, even though I had gotten an A+ in the class.

How do you *do* that? I mean, if you get an A+, for heaven's sake, shouldn't you just automatically and naturally get an "O"? But here was this giant blemish on my otherwise pristine report card. By the time I got home, I was absolutely furious. I raved and I ranted—to the point that my mother made an appointment with the science teacher so that this grievous wrong could be corrected.

In we went. Well, my mother went. Me, I stomped in with folded arms and "indignant" written all over my face. My mother explained that there must have been some mistake in the citizenship grade since I had an A+.

My science teacher smiled and said, "No. There's no mistake."

I could hold back no longer, and I blew a corker. I fairly shouted, "But that's not *fair!* I know more than any other kid in the class. I got an A+! I do better than anybody."

"Yes, that's true," said my science teacher.

"Well, I don't get it!" I sputtered.

Then she sat down in front of me, looked me in the eye, and asked me a very important question. "Merrilee, every day when you're in class, do you do *your* very best?"

I started to talk, and then stopped. "Well, no," I answered

truthfully. I had started to hold back in class because I knew it wasn't cool to be so smart or even so well behaved.

"Are you capable of doing better?" she asked.

I nodded.

"Well then, when you know you are doing your very best, you will get an 'O,'" she responded. And that was that.

Can I tell you how grateful I am for that science teacher? She knew I could do better. And she knew I was also caught up in the trap of comparing myself to others and letting myself off the hook.

That lesson has stayed with me my whole life. I hear my science teacher asking me, "Merrilee, are you doing *your* very best?" And I know that I shouldn't compare myself to anyone else—only to myself and what I am capable of and what the Lord wants me to do.

So I try a little bit harder every day, stretching for the best that is within me.

I learned that when we use anyone else's standards for comparison, we miss out on our own potential that could have been higher. When we *compete,* we are using the performance of others to gauge our own.

Do we hear ourselves?

"But we have to get this house. I'm sick of having the smallest house in the ward."

"I don't know why she does so much; she makes the rest of us look bad."

"But I have to bring something homemade to the potluck, everyone else will."

(Little side note here. I realized that I lived in the perfect ward for me when I went to a potluck we had last year. Every single thing was either bought at Costco or ready-made. There were only maybe three items that were made from scratch. See, these are *my* people. I fit in here! Oh my, is that competitive? I don't think so. Maybe. No, definitely not.)

Can I share a silly conversation? I had made a mistake on some tickets for a performance, thinking I had Saturday tickets when they were, in fact, tickets for Friday. I was exchanging them with the woman who was in charge of tickets. "Oh, I'm so glad you messed up!" she gushed. I stared at her rather incredulously. "You always do everything so perfectly. I feel so much better about myself now."

I was rather taken aback. I turned to her and said quietly, with a tilt of my head, "Gee, I didn't realize we were in a race!"

How bizarre! Why would anyone else's mistakes reflect positively on you or improve your life?

Now what's really odd is that I have this happen to me quite often. (I guess I mess up a lot and make people really happy!)

Since when was a giant race declared? I must have missed the announcement, and yet I see so many women involved in the competition. We compare our marital status, the number of children we have, the callings we have, the money we have or don't have, our size, shape, style, and more!

I find it so odd that we're so competitive over things that don't matter or over which we have no control.

In the end, we only "compete" against ourselves and our own potential—which is limitless. Am I better than I was last year? Did I improve my abilities on that last project? Have I made progress in my relationships? Have I grown? This is truly the only meaningful "competition" we should be engaged in.

Becoming Women of Being

Clearly we can see that comparison—in all its forms, including conformity and competition—can have really negative impacts. We know because we're suffering from them! So how do we change this? How do we go from "Women of Comparison" to "Women of Being"?

Realistically, we may never eliminate all the effects of negative comparisons in our lives, but we can certainly reduce their influence. We can learn to "be." When we simply learn to be ourselves and be true to our unique path in life, we can live with ourselves in the present, aware of our potential and happy with our progress. Simply being.

Step 1: Look at Ourselves with Truth

The first step is to look at ourselves with truth. Oh, this is so easily said and so difficult to do! But we can try.

I have struggled with seeing myself with truth. Throughout my youth, I received many messages that reinforced the opinion that I was unattractive. I did have some challenges as I've mentioned. I wore very thick glasses. I was very tall at a very young age. I was very flat-chested and developed very late. I have figure faults just like every other woman on the planet. And I bought into that opinion completely: "Merrilee is not pretty, cute, or beautiful."

When I look at myself with truth, I realize that I'm not bad. I am actually attractive much of the time. But in my heart of hearts, I have a hard time believing that.

A couple of years ago, I was with my girlfriends, the Ya-Yas, exchanging Christmas gifts. My friend Sue always has a bag of fun items for each of us. That year, she had gotten each of us a hand mirror—the cheap, pink kind with lights around the edge and a picture of a princess on the handle. When you pushed the button, the lights all lit up and a voice said random things like, "You're beautiful!" or "You're a princess!" We all had a great laugh over our priceless, princess mirrors. I took mine home and put it in my bathroom drawer.

The next day, I got ready for the day and then held up the mirror and pushed the button. "You're beautiful!" the voice chimed. I laughed. Then I looked at myself in the mirror with its pretty glow of lights. And you know what? I didn't look too bad!

The next day, I got ready again and grabbed the mirror. "You're wonderful!" the mirror chimed. My husband was in the bathroom and he laughed. "I think you *are* pretty wonderful!" he said. We both laughed some more.

Day after day, I would push the button on that silly mirror.

And day after day, I would look in the mirror and acknowledge that I was a princess!

It was something so small and so silly, but it made an amazing difference in my life. Slowly, I began to look at myself with truth. I was able to silence the negative comparisons in my head for a moment and see reality. I kept that mirror until it was too scratched to even see myself. I'm thinking of buying a new one. What a gift of truth it was to me!

The reality about each of us is truly amazing. When you see yourself with truth, you realize your greatness. You realize your tremendous abilities. You see the light and the power that is within you. You become a Woman of Being, and you come to see and understand who you really are after all. Who are you?

You are a beautiful woman.

You are a good woman.

You are working hard.

You have things to work on.

You are making progress.

You have incredible gifts and talents.

These are truths about you.

Becoming Women of Being is all part of tossing that guilt. We can also toss all the negative voices in our head. Then the joy of who you really are can finally triumph.

In seeing ourselves clearly, we see our divine worth and our divine potential. It is incredible. We can catch the joy of being.

Step 2: Choose to Be Humble

Second, we can reduce comparison in our lives by choosing to be humble. President Ezra Taft Benson encouraged us with these words:

> We can choose to humble ourselves by conquering enmity toward our brothers and sisters, esteeming them as ourselves, and lifting them as high or higher than we are.[6]

We already understand humility on many levels. But to be

Women of Being, we also must choose to be our true selves, without the trappings of mortal standards or success. I've pondered this a great deal. All of us have many gifts and abilities. Some of us have attained success and achievements and honors from the world. How do we handle that? You may have great jobs, great families, great kids, or great talents. How do you react when people compliment you?

I've seen this handled poorly often. In fact, I've handled it poorly a lot, myself.

"You sure gave a great talk!"

"Oh, thanks, but I should have prepared more. I didn't cover half of what I wanted to say."

"I heard you got a promotion. Congratulations!"

"Oh, it's nothing really. They didn't have anyone else to take the job."

This is a sticky question: How do we choose to be humble when we have something to be proud about? I have had a hard time figuring out the answer to that one, and I'm still working on it.

Here are some clues I've discovered so far. One was from a friend of mine, Susan. I stopped by her house one day to see her living room that she had just redecorated. It was absolutely lovely, and I told her so. Her reaction: "Oh, I'm so glad you like it! That means a lot to me!"

I pondered her reaction all the way home. She didn't say, "Oh, it was nothing. I should have hired a decorator because I didn't know what I was doing." She didn't say, "Thanks. I think I did an absolutely outstanding job, don't you?" Instead, she appreciated my appreciation. She moved the focus to me, not herself.

I thought her reaction and her attitude was so inspiring that I began to really pay attention to Susan whenever she got a compliment. And she had a lot to be complimented about—Susan is definitely a Woman of Being! She handled every compliment beautifully every time:

"Your kids are so amazing."

"We sure do love them!" (Focus is on the relationship, not taking credit for other people.)

"You are married to such a fine man!"

"He tries to do his best." (Focus is on him, again not taking credit or boasting.)

"Your backyard turned out great."

"Oh, we had so much fun putting it together." (Focus is on the process, again without a prideful reaction or limiting deflection.)

It was wonderful to study this woman who constantly chose to be humble. She is a woman of grace. She has actively worked to look at herself positively. Susan is comfortable enough with herself to not indulge in either false modesty or rejection of positive feedback. I have learned much from her example.

I discovered another clue from watching Susan's husband, Dave. (I sometimes call him President Dave because not only is he my neighbor and my client, but he was also my stake president!) Dave is a man of accomplishment for whom I have enormous respect. Dave exudes humility, and yet, he is extremely intelligent, extremely capable, and extremely righteous.

So I watched Dave for clues about how to choose to be humble.

For one thing, he was very real. There was no pretense, no posturing whatsoever. I'll never forget passing by his house on my walk and having him launch into a discussion about his upcoming medical procedure. I was surprised that he would discuss it so openly with me, but by the end of our conversation I was laughing so hard! He is truly a man without ego or guile.

Also, I noticed he didn't talk about his accomplishments much. I never heard him going on and on about his work, his projects, his calling. He was content to let others tell his story without feeling the need to toot his own horn.

Finally, I watched as he focused on relationships. External trappings meant nothing to him. He talked equally with yard workers and company presidents. No difference. He gave equal time to a young teen needing to talk or to a family wanting his advice.

I could go on and on with what I learned from observing this humble man.

But honestly, even with what I've learned from my observations, I still struggle sometimes with choosing to be humble. It's hard to walk that tightrope of righteous humility and to do so gracefully!

I have also learned much from studying the life of the Savior. I especially like to read the account of his visit to the Nephites in Third Nephi. Christ takes the time to stand and greet each person there—more than 2,500 individuals—and to allow each one to have a personal experience with him. Such a great lesson on relationships and the importance of people!

Also, I find it very telling that even though he was the Savior of the world, throughout this visit, Christ defers to his Father. In 3 Nephi, chapter 20, the Savior refers constantly to the Father's will. Over and over, he clarifies that this is the Father's plan for us and that he is an instrument in the plan. His attitude is revealing and instructive. The Savior takes time to teach individuals and shows love for each one, but he gives all "credit" to his Father. The Savior's life is a great lesson in humility.

As we choose to cease to compare ourselves to others and as we choose to be humble, we can let go of the focus on self. I find that when I focus on doing my Father's will and on my relationships, I'm not so easily swayed by the comparisons around me. This goes both ways. I'm not so obsessed with my faults because my focus has shifted away from self-absorption, and I can readily give credit to my Father for his blessings to me rather than taking credit for anything I accomplish. The shift away from self immediately and profoundly reduces the negative impacts of comparison.

It is odd that the more we let go of our self-centered focus, the more we are free to actually *be* ourselves. It frees us from the contrived "self" that exists only in comparison to others and allows us to be our real "self" in a loving, humble, accepting way.

Step 3: Look at Others with Charity

A third way to reduce the grip of comparison in our lives is to look at others with charity. One way to do this is to acknowledge that each person is doing the best they can.

As Sheri Dew has said,

> What if we were to each decide that from this time forward we would make just one assumption about each other—that we are each doing the best we can? And what if we were to try a little harder to help each other? Imagine the cumulative effect, not to mention the effect on us spiritually. . . . As we are filled with this love, we no longer feel envy or think evil of others.[7]

That charitable attitude is such a great mental perspective. It frees us from trying to analyze others or to question either their ability or motives. It is such a positive frame of reference that is generous in its scope.

This is also a great attitude to have about ourselves! Too often we give the gift of charity to others, but withhold it from ourselves. Think of the blessing that gift would be to us. Every day the voices in our head begin, "I need to be a better homemaker. This house is a mess." And we can stop them—"I am doing the best I can!"

They start up later in the day. "You should have started earlier on this project." And we can stop them—"I am doing the best I can!"

And they circle on the attack again. "I should have been more patient with her." And we can stop them—"I am doing the best I can!"

There is a great truth that can help us be Women of Being— every day of our lives we wake up and try to do our best! Do you honestly ever wake and say to yourself, "Today I'm going to really try to do a lousy job. I'm going to try to be worse than yesterday." Absolutely not. In fact, I'd go so far as to state that neither you nor I have ever once started out a day that way—ever!

So let's acknowledge that we want to do the best we can. And let's give the gift of charity to others and acknowledge that they, too, are also trying to do the best they can. Indeed, both of these need to be present to have full charity as the Lord has instructed us to "Love thy neighbour as thyself" (Matthew 22:39). Having this outlook takes so much of our comparison mentality and chucks it out the window!

Looking at others with charity also means we should realize that if we knew their story, we might understand them better. I once read a story of a woman who was taught this principle by her parents. As they saw something that would normally cause a person to judge, they would stop and ask, "I wonder what his story is?" She told of a Christmas day when she was a young girl. Her family was traveling to have Christmas dinner with their extended family. They saw a man who was obviously drunk and who had been pulled over by the police. She admitted to feeling disgust for this drunk who had the audacity to be out in such a condition on Christmas day. And then her mother spoke up, "I wonder what his story is?" The family began to discuss what might have caused this man to be in this condition and agreed that he probably had had some terrible sadness in his life and maybe with his family. She said that by the time they passed the man, they were saying a prayer as a family to bless him and help him in his trials. The entire mood in the car had changed into one of love and empathy.

What a powerful question, "I wonder what their story is?"

I met a young woman who is very shy and very withdrawn. "Brittany" is a member of the Church but was inactive for a period of time. Her husband has joined the Church, and they are soon to be sealed in the temple. But there were several things about her that I didn't quite get. I would look at her and think, *There's got to be more to this story and if I knew, I'd understand.*

Well, one day Brittany was in my home for a small get-together and she began to talk. She shared with us that her birth mother was severely schizophrenic and that Brittany and her older sister had repeatedly been in and out of state care until finally the state took them away. They were sent to their birth father, who had remarried. After a time, he kept the older sister, but put Brittany into the foster care system again. She was seven years old. Brittany was taken in by an LDS family as a foster daughter. When she was ten, they offered to adopt her and eventually she was adopted by them. Even after that, there were many trials and struggles.

As she told her story, I was stunned at how hard all that must have been for her. Talk about repeated abandonment! No wonder she was so quiet and private! I was proud of her as well. Through it all, she has hung in there and is now working full-time and attending night school. She is happily married, active in the Church, and recently entered the temple. Incredible! Once I knew her story, I understood her so much better.

Knowing a person's story can help us withhold judgment and extend love and understanding. But there is an even higher level of this principle: simple acceptance.

I call this level of acceptance "looking at people with Christ's eyes." Other people looked at Peter and James and saw fishermen—Christ saw apostles. We see dysfunctional people, depressed people, addicted people, and he sees brothers and sisters whom he loves dearly, people he was willing to suffer and die for.

Sometimes when I meet a person that triggers a reaction of dislike, I'll stop and ask myself, "How would Jesus see this person?" It is amazing how my perception will change. I'm involved in politics and I've found this principle to be invaluable. There are many people I encounter who are less than kind. Often they are very upset about something and may not have all the facts. As I feel myself reacting, I stop and remind myself, "Merrilee, look with Christ's eyes!" I'll mentally step back and look at the person anew. As I do, my entire demeanor softens, and I am filled with love for a person I may barely know.

What's interesting is that when this perceptual shift happens, the entire dynamic changes. I am convinced that the other person immediately feels the change as well. I have been in many situations that were rapidly heating up and the minute I change, they begin to calm.

When we look at people with Christ's eyes—through his filter of complete charity—we begin to see the intrinsic value and goodness of the other person. Things that we never perceived or understood before come to the surface, and the whole cycle of comparison and judgment collapses upon itself. There just isn't any need for it.

Step 4: Remember Our Divine Destiny

A final way to reduce the negative effects of comparison in our lives is to remember who we really are and what our divine destiny really is.

I think we spend a lot of time forgetting this; I know I do.

Last year I taught seminary and my youngest son, Tanner, was in my class. We had several lessons on "remembering" as we discussed the Doctrine and Covenants and the Restoration of the gospel. I taught them over and over to remember where they came from, who they are, and who they were destined to be. It was an amazing year.

After the seminary year ended, Tanner and I were talking one day and I commented on how he had such great self-esteem and confidence—far more than I had had at his age. He looked at me and said, "It's because I remember." I asked him what he meant. "Mom, don't you remember? You taught us over and over that we were destined to be a god. You taught us that's who we really are down deep. Man, I don't need anything more than that to feel good about myself."

I realized he was right. Knowing what we know about who we were and who we are eternally is powerful. Like Tanner, we don't need anything more. And we certainly don't have to compare ourselves to anyone to feel better about ourselves. Once you know you're a queen, what more do you need? You are already a Woman of Being. We just need to remember that!

A great thing happens once we free ourselves from all the comparing, conforming, and competing. We are truly free! We are free to move forward in our unique mission in life.

To catch the joy, we must choose to let go of the chains of comparison.

Satan wants to wrap us in his chains. He whispers in our ear, "You can't do that. You're weak." His greatest desire is to have us doubt ourselves. He asks us, "But how are you compared to her?" and delights when we pause to measure. He discourages us from trying to be like our Savior, telling us, "It's good enough that you're a lot better than your neighbor."

But it's too bad, so sad for Satan. We are far more powerful than he ever will be. We always have been. And we have the power to reject his attempts to destroy us.

When we make the choice to leave behind the world of comparison, we are free to be Women of Being. We are free to mourn with those who mourn (and not say the same thing happened to me!), rejoice with those who rejoice (without having to criticize them to feel better), and comfort those who stand in need of comfort (without secretly feeling put out). We are free to be who *we* are destined to be.

CHAPTER 3

Women of Faith, Not Fear

I always tell people that they can tell what I've struggled with by looking at the topics I write about and speak about. None are more true than this one.

I was born severely cross-eyed. In fact, the story of my surgeries is quite miraculous and should be shared at another time. I began school with thick glasses, one of them sporting a dark red lens. That's just great for fitting in with other children and learning to read and write. As a result of this and many other factors, I was an extremely fearful child.

I was that shy girl who hid behind her mother's skirts. I was afraid of *everything*. And I was deathly afraid of new situations. When school started, I wasn't just nervous the first day. I'd cry for two weeks. I can still remember starting swimming lessons, which I had taken many times before, and still having to leave in the middle of class to walk all the way home because I was so terrified.

When my mom would leave to go out for errands or to the store, I was thrown into a panic and would stand at the window, crying until she returned. It didn't matter if the rest of the family was still home. I was afraid.

I was also afraid of failure. I quit band because I was second chair. I look back on it now and I think how silly I was, quitting because I wasn't number one! I quit the school play because I didn't get cast as the lead. And on and on it went.

I was afraid of what the other kids were saying about me—or worse, what they *weren't* saying because they didn't know I existed. I was afraid of saying the wrong thing or wearing the wrong thing.

And I was deathly afraid of getting hurt or dying. My dad decided to take up skiing when I was about six years old. Every time we went, I cried all the way up the mountain. To this day, when I go skiing, I can feel the panic rise in my throat, and I have to force myself to face it clearly and deal with it. As a result of this almost paralyzing fear, I didn't go on amusement park rides. (Do you know how odd it looks to see a sixteen-year-old young woman on the merry-go-round?) I didn't try diving until I was fourteen.

I grappled with this issue for a very long time. I can remember calling my dad my second year of college, beside myself with fear. My dad helped me work through it.

"Merrilee have you ever failed school?" he asked me.

I giggled. I was at BYU on a four-year academic scholarship. "Well, no," I had to admit.

"Do you like your roommates?"

I had all the same roommates as the year before, and I adored them. "Yes."

He asked me, "Now what exactly are you afraid of?"

I honestly couldn't come up with anything, and slowly the knot in the pit of my stomach began to unwind. I was so used to freaking out at the beginning of a school year, I went into spastic mode without even thinking.

So I suspect by now, you have the picture: "Deathly afraid Chicken Little grows up terrified of own shadow."

I realized at some level that this fear was paralyzing my life, but I felt powerless to do anything about it. On an intellectual level, I realized that most of my fears were irrational and even downright stupid, but that didn't stop them from coming. And I didn't know what to do when they did come. When these kinds of fears wash over you daily like the waves of the sea, you end up like sand. Pulverized.

I was fourteen when I really began to work through my fears. I started working on the issue with the help of the Lord, and he helped me in amazing ways. I made a long list of all the things I was afraid of: swimming, public speaking, failing, roller coasters, Ferris wheels, diving, skiing, being alone, being away from my mom. The list went on and on. And I began attacking those fears one by one. It's interesting that now, over thirty-five years later, I can still remember each confrontation clearly. Those challenges are etched in my memories like crystal.

The first was diving. I was at a campground in Arizona in the deadly heat of summer. Our family was on our way to California. It was late at night, and it was sweltering and my dad and I went to the pool. I remember the low lights and the warm water (which was actually cooler than the warmer air).

"Dad," I said as we stood in the water. "I want to learn to dive, but I'm afraid."

"I know, honey," he said kindly. "Want to give it a try?" He had me sit on the side of the pool and slip in with my hands pointed. After I was comfortable with that, he had me kneel. By the end of our time together, I was diving. And I was also wondering what I had been so afraid of.

Later that summer we were in Utah. Reams grocery store was opening its first Provo store. They had ice cream for ten cents a scoop. I love ice cream. As my brother and I were eating ours, I saw it—a Ferris wheel. Granted, it was a very *tiny* Ferris wheel. I thought, *This is it. It's time.* I asked my brother, who was both younger and braver than I, if he would go with me. We climbed aboard and I breathed deeply. And up we went. My heart was in my stomach. Around we went, and the breeze cooled my face. I laughed, "That's it? That was fun!" We rode that Ferris wheel all afternoon, and I wondered what I had been so afraid of.

On and on through that whole year, I confronted fear after fear.

- Joining the synchronized swim team and looking up from the bottom of the deep pool and realizing, "You did it, girl!"
- Finding myself in front of a huge audience in the school variety show, having them laugh as I launched into an impromptu monologue, and realizing, in that moment, that I really was funny!
- Standing at the top of a high dive for twenty minutes before I was brave enough to jump, and then hearing the applause of all the families who had watched my confrontation and realized what a huge deal it was for me.

On and on, one fear at a time.

And now, I routinely stand to speak in front of thousands of people, and I don't even break a sweat. Now, I adore roller coasters and even have a pool in my backyard. My mother just shakes her head and cannot believe it.

There are still things that make my heart race and my stomach clench. I must admit that "Scaredy-cat Merrilee" sure made a reappearance with a vengeance when I flew in a small plane to Zimbabwe. Trust me, I did a lot of praying and deep breathing on that flight!

Over the years, I have had quite a learning experience with fear, and through it all, I have had a great desire to be a Woman of Faith, not a Woman of Fear.

Norman Vincent Peale gave great advice, "Everybody really knows what to do to have this life filled with joy. What is it? Quit hating people; start liking them. Quit doing wrong, *quit being filled with fear.* Quit thinking about yourself and go out and do something for other people."[1]

Okay, that sounds easy, right? We should just quit being scared! Easier said than done, I'm afraid.

What Are You Afraid Of?

Fear can sometimes be a good thing. It helps us to be cautious in the face of danger. But, as with anything else, sometimes too much of a good thing can be bad.

So what are you afraid of? (Besides the bathroom scale! ☺) Most of us are afraid of failure. We're afraid to go to college because we think we might not make it.

Many of us fear failure when we receive a new Church calling. I know I do. Let's just say that homemaking is not one of my strengths, so when they called me as the Homemaking counselor, I literally burst out laughing and asked if it was some kind of joke.

Many of us are afraid of failing at work, which can be quite a serious concern if we are supporting a family.

I worry that I might be a failure as a mother. Being a parent is such a difficult job and failure has such serious consequences. We fear how our children will turn out or what they'll encounter.

The Church is filled with Saints who worry that they might fail at the ultimate test of mortality—Will I make it to the top of the celestial kingdom or will I fail?

We're also afraid of the unknown. Moving can be a terrifying venture. And what if we never get married? Or what if our marriage fails? We worry about choices our children or spouses will make in the future. We fear the future of the stock market, the future of the country, and the future of our waistline. What will happen?

And who can be alive in this day and age and not fear evil? It seems to surround us on all fronts, and no one is immune. I'm to the point where I can hardly watch the news or read the newspaper anymore. The evil and filth and violence seem to be everywhere. We also fear the effects of evil on our family members. Pornography, immorality, drugs, and other evils reach their pernicious grasp into our very homes. Any person who has ever read a paper, watched the news, or read the scriptures fears evil. What will Satan pull next?

And comparing this world that my children are growing up in to the world I grew up in is terrifying. I wonder what my grandchildren will have to face. How can we survive morally and physically in a world where evil is not only tolerated but applauded and displayed on the big screen? What if someone tries to carjack me or breaks into my house? Should I pull over and help that stranded motorist or are they a serial killer on the loose? These are real fears and concerns of people everywhere. How will we be affected by the growing evil in the world?

We also fear physical impairment or injury. I have many elderly clients who live in perpetual fear of falling and breaking a leg or a hip. We all flock to get every shot and every vaccine so we can stave off illness of every kind. Will we get cancer? Have a heart attack? These fears loom over all our lives.

But I believe the biggest fear we all share is far more basic: We are afraid of what other people think of us. Bottom line. It's rather pathetic, I know, but every single one of us has this fear. Every sister in the Church gets nervous when the visiting teachers come. Is the house clean enough? Do I look okay? Will the children behave?

We are afraid of what others think when our children have temper tantrums in the store. We're afraid that coworkers might be critical of our performance. We scour the fashion magazines to make sure that we look "just so," so no one can fault our appearance. And if we are overweight, it is a constant obsession to conform to the "thin" norm so that others will not be critical of us. Will our neighbors, family members, ward members judge us? What will they think? These fears constantly creep into our thinking like a pernicious cancer of confidence.

The list of fears could be endless. I've tried to summarize the big ones to help us identify what we're dealing with.

So why are we afraid of all these things?

I think we feel fear most when we cannot control the outcome. We can't control other people, so we feel vulnerable.

Effects of Fear

Living as a Woman of Fear has terrible effects on our lives. Probably the most prevalent is inaction. We are so afraid that we don't *do* anything. I've received e-mail after e-mail from women gripped in the paralysis of fear. One woman asserts over and over, "I can't do it. I won't do it." And then she doesn't go on the blind date. Another doesn't apply for the dream job. And still another rejects the Church calling. Much safer to do nothing, they believe.

Many women suffer from depression as a result of the grip of fear in their lives. Fear creates a disconnect between what they really *want* to do (which is something) versus what they *are* doing (which is nothing) because they are afraid. Who wouldn't be depressed over that? Crying, failure to engage in life, sleeping too much, and many more behaviors in the spectrum of depression can indicate that fear is present.

Growing up, I was so overwhelmed with constant and daily fear, that I was often depressed. As you can probably guess, this turns into a vicious cycle of fear leading to depression leading to more fear. It is a difficult cycle to break.

Sin is another side effect of fear. Now, this one may puzzle you a bit, but think about it for a moment. How many of us have done something we didn't want to do, that we knew was wrong, just because we were afraid of what other people would think?

Many teens (and I believe many adults) are so afraid of facing the "what will they think" situation that they bend their own moral code and engage in sinful behaviors of all varieties. I remember a woman who was married to a nonmember. She was so afraid of other people's judgment in social situations that she would drink a glass of wine at every party in order to fit in. Another woman was so afraid of being alone that she engaged in immoral behaviors so she wouldn't feel lonely. We may have habits in our families or in our social customs that may be leading us to succumb to sin simply because we fear to be different. Or, we can be so afraid of change, especially in ourselves, that we continue in sin rather than repent.

Our decision-making ability takes a big hit when we give in to fear. We may not leave an unhealthy, abusive marriage even if it's for the best because we're afraid of the financial, emotional, or physical consequences. We may not take the great job offer even though it would be a tremendous opportunity because we're afraid of having to learn a new skill. Fear can color and cloud our thinking to the point where poor judgment reigns.

This leads us to a cumulative negative impact of fear: stifled growth. When we let fear set up huge roadblocks in our lives, we cannot become who we are destined to be. We close doors, shut windows, and sit stagnant in our tiny comfortable world, in our safe little circle, and wonder why we are not as happy as we want to be. Oh, the lost opportunities! Oh, the lost growth! As John Greenleaf Whittier wrote:

> *Of all sad words of tongue and pen*
> *The saddest are these: "It might have been!"*[2]

In fact, a Woman of Fear faces what I call "The Guilt of the Undone." She's afraid of computers and new technology so she doesn't work on her family history. And then she feels guilty about it. She doesn't call her elderly mother because she's afraid of the onslaught—"Why aren't you married yet? Are you dating?" or "When are you going to get those kids under control?" or "Haven't you pulled your house together yet? In my day a woman wouldn't be caught dead with a house like that." So she doesn't call her mother. And then she feels guilty about it.

I recall a fast and testimony meeting in January many years ago. A woman stood and said that she had set a goal for the new year: "I want to live this year with no regrets." That struck me. She expanded, "I want to say the things I should say to people, especially tell those I love that I do love them. I want to try the things I want to try and not look back at the end of the year and wonder why I didn't. I want to stop doing the things I don't want to do. I just want to look back on this year and say, 'I did it! No regrets.'" That goal has stuck with me ever since. What a brave, bold way of living! What a great way to ditch the fear and toss the guilt!

Courage

We've admitted that we are, at times, Women of Fear and that we all really want to be Women of Faith. So how can we work to reduce the fear in our lives? What can we do about it?

We can have courage.

Mary Fisher, AIDS activist who had contracted HIV from her husband, spoke at the 1992 Republican Party Convention, "I don't want my children to think, as I once did, that courage is the absence of fear; I want them to know that courage is the strength to act wisely when we are most afraid."[3]

Deuteronomy 31:6 holds great encouragement, "Be strong and of a good courage, fear not, nor be afraid of them: for the Lord thy God, he it is that doth go with thee; he will not fail thee, nor forsake thee."

I love how Dorothy Bernard described it: "Courage is fear that has said its prayers."[4]

Each of us can seek to develop that kind of courage. Each of us can acknowledge that yes, we have fear, but we are strong enough to choose to act despite that fear. Each of us can become Women of Faith who choose to act with courage.

Battle Plan

So let's begin to fight the fears that grip us. Let's put together a battle plan to do so. And congratulations! You are now the general of your own life! Every good general puts together a battle plan before he goes to war and the same holds true for each of us. We need to have a plan.

I'll share with you some ideas and skills that I have learned, and hopefully, they will help you take those first steps to aggressively tackle your own fears.

Step 1: Name the Enemy

What Am I Afraid Of?

You cannot fight an unknown enemy. So start by saying it out loud. Admit it.

- "I'm afraid of applying for school."
- "I'm afraid of public humiliation by my children." (Amen!)
- "I'm afraid of getting a divorce."

Admit it to yourself first. And then admit it to someone you trust. There is something powerful in sharing our fears with others. It gets that boogeyman out of the closet where we can see it clearly.

Sisters have shared several fears with me:

- "I'm afraid of groups. I have to have an empty seat next to me to feel comfortable. And please don't ask me to pray or speak!"
- "I'm afraid that if I tell my boyfriend I want to get married, he'll bolt."
- "I'm afraid of starting my own business. I've never done anything like this before."
- "I know my son is doing drugs, but I'm afraid to confront him. What if he moves out? I think that will be the end of his involvement with the Church."
- "I'm afraid of sending my daughter to preschool. Will she be safe?"

These are just a few fears. And these women have already fought half the battle by admitting their fear. This first step is so powerful. They've been able to identify the fear clearly and to share it with another person.

I take this same step often. I begin most days with a long walk where I pray and ponder. I'll be on my prayer/walk and I'll think, *Gee, why am I not moving forward on this problem or issue?* and bam! I'll stop in my tracks because I recognize that telltale sign. "Okay, Merrilee, what are you afraid of?" I'll say to myself. (And yes, I talk out loud on my daily walks. I think most of my neighbors wonder about me. They'll ask me, "Are you practicing a lecture? I see you talking a lot when you're walking." It's better now because people assume I have a cell phone earpiece.)

After you have verbally acknowledged your fear, it's equally powerful to write it down. Somehow seeing it on paper (or on a computer screen) makes it real. And you now have a visual starting point.

Perhaps the most crucial part of this step is to have a heart-to-heart prayer with Heavenly Father and admit your fears to him. Just tell him sincerely what it is that's in your way and ask for his help.

Step 2: Describe the Enemy

Why Am I Afraid?

After you have identified your fear, explore it a little. Ask yourself, "Why am I afraid of that?"

Perhaps you identified that you were afraid to ask for a promotion. As you then ask yourself *why* you're afraid of that, you may discover that there can be many sides to this fear. Perhaps you're afraid that you may not be able to do the work required well enough. Or maybe you're afraid that your coworkers will snub you and it will cost you their friendship. Finally, it may be that you fear the time constraints of the promotion may take away from the time you spend with your family.

Many people are afraid of public speaking because they fear public embarrassment. What if they say something stupid? I mean, what if they say something really, really dumb. It could happen. I should know—I do it routinely. (We all have gifts. Mine is putting my foot in my mouth on stage. Yes, that's figurative.)

Others may fear quitting a full-time job to be home with their children. When they ask this second question of *why* they're afraid, they identify other facets.

- "What if we can't handle it financially?"
- "What if my husband loses his job?"
- "Being home full-time sounds so incredibly boring; how will I stand it?"
- "My entire neighborhood is going to think I'm crazy. I'll be the only stay-at-home mom here!"
- "My husband doesn't want me to quit. If I do, will it put too much of a strain on our marriage?"

The importance of asking this question of *why* is that there may be other factors at play that need to be faced. As you explore your fear you'll realize, "Wow, there's more to this than I thought!" You'll understand the entire spectrum of your fear and all the elements you're facing. This may sound like it's making things worse but in fact, the opposite is true. Once the fear is out there in all its glory, then you can really begin to handle it and make progress.

Before, you always knew that things were lurking behind hidden doors and that made it even more frightening. Now it's all out. You can see how big, how wide, and how deep it is. And often a fascinating thing will happen. As you describe your enemy more fully, you may realize that your true fear is actually different from the one you initially stated.

For example, you thought you were afraid of asking for a promotion, but when you went through this step, you realized that what you are really afraid of is losing the friendships you've developed over the years with your coworkers. Knowing this, you can address *that* fear first, and then pursue your dream.

If we don't take this second step in our battle plan, we often waste a lot of time addressing fears that are not at the root of the problem. It's like trimming a weed. The weed may look better, but the stupid thing keeps growing!

For years my friend struggled in a lousy marriage. She was working two jobs to support a husband who couldn't seem to find a job. She put up with his negativity toward her Church activity, which became a moot point after she took on that second job and quit going to Church at all. Then, she felt the loss of the gospel in her life and the loss of social support from her ward that she had always enjoyed. But she was afraid a divorce would trigger too many family and financial issues. So, she endured decades of misery.

A few months ago, her husband left her. I sat down with her to go through the finances that he had left in complete shambles. She realized she would have to file for bankruptcy to deal with all the credit cards he had secretly opened and maxed out. And as we sat together, she acknowledged that she could and would weather this financial catastrophe.

Then she looked at me and in a small voice said, "But I'm afraid of being alone."

I realized then, as did she, that this was her true fear. She didn't want to be alone. And yet she had spent years scrambling to address her financial fears and concerns. As a result, she had lost many relationships and social connections that would have helped her minimize the feelings of loneliness she now faces.

Defining your enemy and all its layers is a crucial step in addressing your true fears.

Step 3: Risk Assessment

What Is the Worst Possible Thing That Could Happen?

Every good general puts together a strategic plan, including a thorough risk assessment, before going to war. After assessing the risks, the strategic plan of addressing those threats can then be formulated. The same holds true for us.

After we have identified the real fear, we can then ask, "What is the worst possible thing that could happen?" This is the risk assessment.

My husband would like me to join him in his beloved hobby of scuba diving. I have no desire to do so. And so we had this conversation.

"Honey," I said, "I know that you want me to go scuba diving with you, but it has a pretty big downside."

"Really, like what?"

"Well, I could *die*." Hmmmmm. That's a pretty *bad* thing that could happen, is it not? I rest my case.

If you're asked to help with making calls to raise money for the PTA event, what is the worst possible thing that could happen? The person on the other end of the phone could say "No." My, my, that's horrible. Well, I supposed they could say, "No, and don't ever call me again." Okay . . .

We have a neighbor with a very annoying dog who barks a lot. What is the worst possible thing that could happen if we confronted the neighbor? The very worst thing is that they would shun us forever. Now frankly, this neighbor is already shunning us because politically I am a staunch conservative and they are die-hard liberals. I figure we don't have a lot to lose on this one.

I have to admit that I had to develop a battle plan for my trip to Africa with our favorite charity, Mothers without Borders. I would be going on a team expedition to Zambia and Zimbabwe for almost three weeks. And I was scared. Let's face it. I got to this point and asked this question and the answers I came up with were very scary! I could face disease—really *bad* diseases. The plane could crash sometime in the thirty hours it would take to get there! I could be attacked while I was in Africa.

However, there is a second step to this process. After we ask "What is the worst possible thing that could happen?" we then have to determine probability. We ask, "How likely is it that this worst possible thing will occur?" Then we can decide if we are willing to tackle this particular fear.

I had to admit, people rarely die while scuba diving. The likelihood of me passing away while driving my car in my neighborhood is actually much higher. So while I feel scuba diving has a tremendous downside, the likelihood of my underwater death is almost nil.

The risk could be higher. If you're making a fundraising call, it's likely that the "no" answer would show up often—maybe half the time. But if you were calling mostly friends, the odds would be less—maybe only a quarter of the time. Can you handle getting rejected half the time, knowing that you'll get a "yes" the other half?

I used this method all the time when I was dealing with my fear of roller coasters. I would look at the line of people coming off the ride and think, "Now look, Merrilee, none of them died." It was silly, but it worked!

As we look at the answers to these two questions—What is the worst that could happen? and How likely is it?—we will reveal some of our irrational fears. You may fear leading music in sacrament meeting. What's the worst possible thing that could happen? Your slip could fall down, perhaps. Not too likely.

For a while, I had a fear of feeding the missionaries. Now this was with good reason. One day I fed them stroganoff, and one missionary took one look at it and said, "What in the world is *this?* My mother would *never* serve this." The other missionary kicked him under the table. "Well, weren't you lucky," I said sweetly.

But as I was pondering my fear of feeding the missionaries, I realized that I could develop a strategic plan. What if I served them pizza every time they came for dinner? What was the probability of them criticizing pizza? I decided it was almost nil. Hence, I have bought pizza for the missionaries ever since, and my fears have evaporated.

(Please note that I said "almost nil" and not zero. This is because one day another missionary said, "Pizza again?" I explained that I was a lousy cook and a busy woman and figured all missionaries loved pizza. "Well, you could give it more effort," he muttered. I looked at the Costco pizza on paper plates and the unopened bag of salad still on the table and realized, *Well, he's right—I could.* Then I thought for a moment. Nah . . . I figure those guys are lucky I'm still feeding them!)

Many times, when we have to actually look at the worst thing that could happen, we realize it isn't really very likely after all. I've used this technique with my children over the years. They're afraid to go to school. I'll start with the outrageous. "What's the worst possible thing that could happen? Will the teacher chew on your leg?" They giggle a bit. "Or a spider could eat the school!" By then they're laughing. The situation is diffused and we can sit down and realize that the worst possible thing is certainly very minor.

Also, as we go through these two steps we will further define what we're facing and why we're afraid. Anna is afraid to tell her sister she can't spend the night at Anna's house with her boyfriend.

As Anna goes through this strategic planning and risk assessment, she realizes that she's afraid because it's possible that her sister will completely cut off contact with her. That's a serious concern! But as she looks at the probability of that happening, Anna realizes that it is extremely unlikely and is willing to risk telling her sister of her decision.

Gabrielle, on the other hand, has determined that she is afraid of skydiving with her adventurous girlfriends. As she goes through these questions, she realizes that the likelihood of injury or death is higher than she is willing to risk because she is a single mom.

Looking at each of these aspects helps us to see the whole picture and deal with its elements.

Step 4: Develop Your Tactical Plan

What If?

So we've gone through several steps: We know what it is we're afraid of; we have explored why we're afraid of it; we've identified what the worst possible thing is that could happen and how likely it is to happen.

It's time for the next step. What if it happens? What if that really bad thing actually happens? Or what if all those lesser bad things happen instead? What then?

This is the preparation aspect of our battle plan. This is where we make our contingency plans. Any good general will address this necessary step. What if the enemy drops bombs? What if the enemy uses chemical weapons? What if they use their air support, naval support, or ground troops?

It is the same for us. Each of us can face our fears better if we are well prepared. Each of us needs to prepare and develop our plans to conquer our fears. The Lord reassures us of this repeatedly throughout the scriptures: "But if ye are prepared ye shall not fear" (D&C 38:30)

You may fear skiing. After all, what if you break your leg?

65

Alright, you can develop a tactical plan and be prepared. "I'll have my husband handle the carpool and grocery shopping."

You may fear asking for a raise. What if you get turned down? Your plan may include writing a follow-up letter and telling your boss, "I appreciate the time you spent with me, and I want to assure you that I will be working toward qualifying for the raise I'm requesting. I'll work on items 1, 2, and 3 that we discussed. I'd like to meet with you again in six months to assess my progress toward this raise. Thank you for your feedback. I'm committed to the company and to bettering myself." Can you imagine? Your boss would have a heart attack! He would expect you to be upset, to quit, to be depressed, or worse. And instead, here you had this great plan and were ready to continue to pursue your goal fearlessly. I would think that when you go back in six months with all of the items addressed, your boss would be highly inclined to give you that raise! All because you had your plan in place in advance to address your fear.

Perhaps you live in fear that your husband may die and you would be left unable to cope. So let's build a basic plan. You would need financial preparation (life insurance, savings, etc.), and you would need career planning (education, training, networking). You may also need to develop a support system within the family, Church, and community so that you would have a net to fall back on. Finally, you may need to address issues with respect to the children. Are you starting to see how a woman who faces this fear head-on and addresses it is so much more well-prepared? Now I hope a wife would never look forward to the death of her husband, but I hope she would not be deathly afraid of it either with this safety net firmly in place.

I am an estate planning attorney by trade and have dealt with many women over the years who have had a variety of preparation. One woman had literally never written a check in her life. (Talk about a severe lack of preparation!) I urged her terminally-ill husband to sit down with her and review their finances, but he refused, and she wouldn't ask. He just told her to open the briefcase in his office. Well, when he died, she did open that brief-case and discovered that he had taken out a second mortgage, gut-ted out the equity in their home, and had racked up over $50,000 in credit card debt. She had to immediately sell her home and move to a remote area with a lower cost of living. All because she was too afraid to plan. Yet, when she came to a point where her fears became irrelevant—she had to act.

Then there was Judy. Judy didn't know much about finances, so she joined a women's investment club and learned a great deal. She reviewed and updated her and her husband's life insurance and savings. She stayed involved in the business affairs of her husband and in the management of their home. She got their trust and wills done. She was active in her church and her community and had many friends. When her very successful husband died in his early 60s, Judy was prepared and handled it extremely well. I remember her sitting on my couch to review the estate one last time and hav-ing her say, "That's it? That was so easy!" I assured her it was easy because she had prepared so well.

I must say, as an estate planning attorney I am constantly amazed at how many people say, "Gee, I never thought about that." Part of me wants to say, "What? You've never thought about dying? Isn't that like a 100% probability?" What they're actually saying is that they've thought about it, but have never wanted to face it or prepare for it.

It is crucially important to teach this planning step to your chil-dren. A great way is to play the "What If?" game with your chil-dren at family home evening. This is wonderful for emergency preparedness as well.

- "What if a stranger grabs your arm?" Then you talk through exactly what they are to do.
- "What if the house catches on fire?" Then you all practice crawling outside and meeting on the sidewalk.
- "What if you go in the kitchen and Mommy is on the floor and won't answer you?" Then you practice dialing 9–1–1 on

the phone. (Quick tip: unplug it first. I learned this the hard way.)

- "What if Daddy loses his job?" Then you show them the pantry full of your year's supply. (We've had to use ours twice now for almost a year each time.)

You may argue that you don't want to freak out your kids. But I see so many parents who overprotect their children and then wonder why they are so lacking in coping skills. It is remarkable how much better children can handle their fears when they know the plan! Then they'll have coping skills. They'll know what to do.

We went through this process with my youngest son, Tanner. Tanner was going to first grade and had just started wearing glasses. He was very afraid of going to school with his new glasses, so we talked him through the process.

"What are you afraid of?"

"I'm afraid of going to school," he said.

"What is it about going to school that you're afraid of?"

"Well, I'm afraid that my teacher will make a big deal out of my glasses, and I'm afraid the kids will laugh at me."

"Anything else?"

"Well, yeah. What if my glasses get broken at recess? They cost a lot of money and you'll be mad. Or what if I lose them?"

And so we began to assess each item and whether it was likely to occur. We agreed that most of them were definitely possible.

Then we began to develop Tanner's tactical plan. After talking it through, he decided that he would go to class with his glasses in their carrying case. He would go early and talk to the teacher and tell her that he was wearing glasses now and that he hoped she wouldn't make a big deal out of it. We asked him, "Do you want us to help you with that?" He assured us that he could handle it on his own. Then, he would wear the glasses for the first few days only during reading or when he couldn't see, and he would gradually increase his wearing time. He also developed "come-backs" to say if he got teased. After we were done, we asked him, "Are you ready to handle this?" He assured us that he was.

Off he went to school with glasses in tow. When he came home, we asked him how it went. "Well, I talked to the teacher and she was fine. Then I put them on during reading. I forgot to take them off and just kept wearing them. One kid asked me when I started wearing glasses, and I told him this summer. It went fine." And that was it. The preparation had equipped him to face what had happened and to squelch his fears before they stopped him.

Another powerful tool in tactical planning is through role-playing. For example, you can take on the role of the class bully and have your two daughters practice how they would handle peer pressure. Role-playing even works well with adults! I do it often with myself as I work through events and situations mentally before I go through them in reality.

Preparation can eliminate the paralysis of fear in miraculous ways. It is definitely worth the effort.

Step 5: Identify Your Troops and Resources

Who or What Will Help Me?

No matter how hard you work on preparation, some fears cannot and should not be tackled alone. Do you think a general would run out onto the battlefield by himself? Never happen. A good general knows exactly how many troops he has and what resources he can draw on.

It is crucial that we do the same. So ask yourself, "Who will help me?" You will probably be amazed at the answer. As you put together your plan to attack your fear, you can and should enlist the help of others, including family, friends, and professionals. But how do you *do* that? Most women feel guilty asking anybody to help them with anything.

Let's say you're teaching Gospel Doctrine during the year we study the Old Testament. Now there's a scary situation! But what if you started your first class by saying, "You know. I've never done this before, and it's a little scary for me. I'd appreciate everyone contributing a lot, and if you ask me something we can't figure out, I'll study and come back with the answer next week." Imagine how the class would react.

First of all, they're glad *they* don't have to teach, so they will be understanding. Second, those who do know a lot about the subject will be excited to have input. And those who don't know a lot about the Old Testament will feel better because they know you're in the same boat and that you are willing to learn. I suspect that few in the class would sit in judgment of you for your honesty, and that instead people would be willing to help you.

So the first step in rallying the troops is to simply state that you're afraid and that you need help! You might be surprised at how many people will naturally want to help you. Wouldn't you want to help?

Another way is to create a mutual support situation. Perhaps you're trying to exercise and you're afraid you won't stick to a program. What a great opportunity to ask, "Who will help me?" You can get the help of friends or family to join with you or encourage you. You can join a class, which is essentially a pre-structured support group! Bingo—automatic help! You are helping the people on your team and they're helping you. A mutual support system can leave you better equipped to tackle your fear.

Sometimes you just need to put it out there that you're seeking help. It can be as easy as saying, "I'm going to be starting a youth theater camp, and I'll be looking for people to help run the camp." I've done this myself. I have run for political office twice (I even won the second time!) and will be running again this year. I rely heavily on volunteers for help and support. To start, I announce that I'm running and simply state that I need help with the campaign. All kinds of people come forward to help because it's something they're interested in or they believe in me. Often people are grateful that you are brave enough to step up and be in charge.

If you are looking for a job, enlisting the help of others is critical. Tap into your entire network of relationships and then ask them to tap into their networks as well. On and on you build.

In addition to troops, a general needs to be aware of what resources he has. So ask yourself, "What will help me?"

To identify your resources, begin by looking around you at what is available. You may gather information, seek out experts, or identify skills you or others may have that will help you.

For example, many years ago I wanted to have LASIK eye surgery. Always a little scary to have eye surgery. Especially because I had six eye surgeries when I was a child. I began by gathering pamphlets with information and reading them, as well as researching extensively on the Internet. I identified friends and acquaintances who had had the surgery and talked to all of them. Then I talked to friends in the medical field. Finally, I interviewed three different eye doctors who did this type of surgery. I had many resources at my disposal. After drawing on all of them, I was able to move past my fears and pick an excellent surgeon and have the procedure.

Another example would be retirement planning. In my law practice, I meet with many clients, and when I bring up the subject of retirement planning, I can see the fear in their eyes right away. Recently, I had clients in their mid-50s who were way behind in their retirement savings. I began to list for them a battery of resources—financial planners, an accountant, a life insurance agent—and then I reviewed their estate planning, which was my element. I urged them to meet with these individuals immediately so that they would be prepared. The woman indicated that she had just signed up for a retirement preparation class, and I told her that was a great first step. But they were stuck on facing this issue because they had not yet marshaled their resources.

My son and new daughter-in-law recently bought a new house. (Yeah! We finally have a girl in the family!) Buying a house can be a scary step, but when they started the process, they began lining up their resources: a realtor, a lender, an insurance agent, and seasoned parents. As they went through the process, they were very careful to research options on the Internet and talk to friends and advisors. All of these resources were enormously important in addressing what could have been a frightening process.

When you are identifying your troops and resources, it is crucial to ASK, ASK, ASK. I had very wise clients who, once we were done, asked the question, "Is there anything that we haven't asked about that we should have?" What a great question!

Ask for information.

Ask for ideas.

Ask for referrals.

Ask for help.

Ask for opinions and advice.

People will respond when you ask for help, and you will be armed with resources to face the fearful situations you encounter.

My friend Kathy Headlee shared with me a great mind-set that she had learned. She said to think, "Every person I meet is willing to help me." That's a rather bold mind-set, but it is amazingly effective.

Kathy is the president of Mothers without Borders; I am on the board of directors and recently, I sat in a training meeting Kathy held in Zimbabwe. We had traveled there to meet with a small group of amazing women. Kathy explained that she had met with these women on a prior trip to Zimbabwe in order to help Lettie and her friends face the seemingly impossible task of feeding two hundred orphans a day with only five large pots over a wood fire. Their sweet efforts of caring and love had grown considerably, and they were learning how to deal with a totally new experience in their lives.

Initially, the women had thought, "Oh, how can we do this? No one will help!" They were overwhelmed and couldn't imagine anyone agreeing to help them with this enormous task. Kathy taught them to think, "Every person I meet is willing to help me!" We had returned to Zimbabwe several months later to meet with the women and receive their report.

As the secretary stood to give her report, she began, "We were taught to think, 'Every person I meet is willing to help me!'" She smiled shyly at Kathy. "And so we prayed to God, and he sent us a miracle!" The women asked the miller if they could have his left-over grindings, and he agreed. So now they have free cornmeal from the miller for all the children. They approached the school and asked for uniforms, and their request was granted. They asked the grocer for free oranges, and now the children have nutritious oranges every day. "It's true," reported the secretary. "Everybody *is* willing to help us! And here you are from America to help us!" It was a moving experience as I learned the power of asking with the expectation of help.

Normally, we go through life believing that nobody wants to help us. How many times have we said, "I know you're busy, but . . ." We just set ourselves up for an immediate negative reaction with that kind of thinking. People say this to me constantly. Some sisters once needed me to accompany them on the piano. Their first words were, "Well, we know you're really, really busy, but . . ." That approach always puts me in a difficult spot. Yes, I am really, really busy, but that does not mean I'm not willing to help.

Contrast that with this request: "Merrilee, I know you'll help me. We need a speaker for our conference." Though I was unable to speak, I was able to give them a referral and contact information for another speaker. "See," my friend said, "I knew you would help." I was so happy to be able to act as a resource. It only took moments, but help was delivered and good feelings prevailed.

Do not be afraid to ask. People love to help others. Give them a chance to help you! You know that you would help them if they asked, wouldn't you?

Step 6: Finalize Your Battle Plan

Where Do I Start?

You've made great progress on tackling your fears! You've identified them and defined them. You've asked what could happen that you're afraid of, and you've asked how you can be prepared for those outcomes. Now it's time to go to battle!

To finalize your battle plan, sit down with some paper and ask, "In order to deal with this fear, what do I need to *do* first?" Pause and think about this carefully. Then identify all the steps it will take for you to do it—to work through this fear you have.

After you have identified specific steps, set a timeframe goal for each one.

Let's say you're afraid of going back to school, but you really want or need to do it. What is the first step? Some may say, "Well, pick a major." Others may think, "You need to apply." But think carefully and specifically. Think of something very small. Probably, the first step is simply to pick out a school. So your list might look like this:

1. Go on the Internet and look at Palomar College. (I picked this because it's close to where I live.)
2. Go on the Internet and look at Mesa College.
3. Compare the two and decide on a college.
4. Pick up an application (or more likely, go online and print the application!).
5. Go to the counseling office and meet with a counselor.
6. Fill out the application.
7. Request transcripts from high school.
8. Get five letters of recommendation.

And on and on you would go, identifying each small, specific, and attainable step.

Note step 1 isn't, "Apply to college." That's way too scary and overwhelming! But broken down, each step is easier to manage; you can start and finish in a fairly brief amount of time.

Remember to set a time goal for each step. Start with the first one and attach a time limit. "I will go online and look at Palomar College *within one week*." That is a clear goal and you could probably accomplish that within one week, right? Not too scary.

"I will go online at look at Mesa College *within one week after* I look at Palomar." Again, very doable. On and on you would go.

After you have your battle plan finalized with all the steps and the amount of time you want to allow for each one, you come to the most important part.

You must focus *immense* effort on step 1. Taking the first step is the hardest part of facing your fears. Just keep in mind your goal: "I will *focus immense effort.*" Keep repeating that if you have to. And give it every ounce of your effort. You'll find after you do the first step, the rest will come far more easily.

I suspect you've experienced this before with something you've been procrastinating (which is just a code word for "I'm afraid to do it!"), and that when you finally just *started,* the rest was easy.

Too often people don't start because they've made that first step too huge in their minds. It's far easier to step up four inches than it is to step up four feet! So just make that first step really small and really easy to do.

Battlefield Preparation—"Act As If"

While you're getting ready to take that first step, it's a great idea to prepare your battlefield.

Many years ago I was attending a conference before starting my freshman year at BYU. I walked through the Wilkinson Center and noticed a huge class going on in the ballroom. Out of curiosity, I sat in a chair on the back row. Now you need to know what condition I was in. Take "fearful young woman" and add "first year at BYU, far away from home" and you get the picture. I was a wreck. Weeping, wailing, gnashing of teeth—you got it. And I was praying like mad.

The teacher was Don Black. Brother Black asked a young man to come up on stage. He whispered in the young man's ear. The boy walked across the stage, looking at his shoes, with shoulders slumped and head bowed. Then Brother Black whispered in his ear again, and the same boy walked back across the stage waving, smiling, calling out "Hello!" Brother Black asked the audience,

"Which boy would you talk to and be friends with?" Well, everybody said the second one, of course. We didn't want to interrupt the first boy's pity-party.

And then Brother Black asked a question that changed my life forever in an instant.

"Which one is his *real* personality?"

Hmmmmm. We didn't know. We had no clue. We had never met the boy. And yet, if he acted outgoing, we would treat him as if he were outgoing. If he acted shy, we would treat him as if he were shy. We didn't know which was his real personality.

Brother Black then taught us about the "Act As If Principle." If you act as if you were a certain way, people will treat you that way. And eventually, you will become that way.

I cannot tell you how profound an experience that was for me. It was like the heavens opened and a conduit of pure light just beamed down into my head. I got it. I totally got it.

I walked out of that class a changed person. I decided at that very moment to begin this grand experiment with my life. I was a shy, repressed, depressed person. But I could pretend!

I can remember so distinctly walking across campus, smiling and waving at people. I could act, and I was acting up a storm. I was the most friendly freshman on the planet.

I had a marriage proposal in three days. I kid you not. And no, I didn't marry him. Who proposes in three days? But for a young woman who probably had three dates in high school, it was astounding.

So if you want to be a strong, confident woman, act as if you're a strong, confident woman. Pretend if you need to! People will begin to interact with you as if you are. I use this principle all the time in my own life.

Let's say you're afraid to go back to school, as we mentioned. Act as if you're a brilliant student. What do brilliant students do? Do it!

Let's say you're afraid to ask for a promotion. Act as if you're the best employee the company has ever seen. What do highly capable employees do? Do it!

Let's say you're afraid to teach Relief Society. Act as if you're the best teacher ever. What do great teachers do? Do it!

You may think this sounds simplistic, but I must testify from the depths of my soul of the power of this principle. I know because I have used it for decades and have seen amazing results. I am largely who I am today because of it.

We've been taught this principle all our lives. We've been taught that we are to try to become like Christ, and he tells us how. *Act as* he would. Pure and simple. And powerful.

Our "battlefield" is then prepared. We can see the lay of the land. We know how we need to act. And we can "act as if" if necessary.

Step 7: Add Your Primary Advisor

The Savior

As we strive to transform from Women of Fear into Women of Faith, it is not enough to just work on these six steps. To help us eliminate or confront our fears we must take the final step to become Women of Faith. We must increase our faith. In a simple analogy, if we pull weeds, it's important to plant flowers in their place or the weeds will return.

To increase our faith, we must add a consultant to our plan— our Savior, Jesus Christ. We must turn to him to truly become Women of Faith.

We should have faith. But faith in what?

First, we can have absolute faith that the Lord is there. The Lord says, "Be of good cheer, and do not fear, for I the Lord am with you, and will stand by you; and ye shall bear record of me, even Jesus Christ, that I am the Son of the living God, that I was, that I am, and that I am to come" (D&C 68:6).

To me, it is one of the absolute greatest miracles ever that my Heavenly Father and my Savior know ME. Among the billions and zillions of his children, God knows me by name, personally. Isn't that amazing? And they know you too!

I testify that Heavenly Father is there. Your Savior is there, and the Lord will stand by you and never abandon you.

Second, we can have faith that Heavenly Father loves us and answers our prayers. Elder Neal A. Maxwell explained, "The acceptance of the reality that we are in the Lord's hands is only a recognition that we have never really been anywhere else."[5]

The Lord is bold to promise us that he will answer our prayers. He has said, "I, the Lord, am bound when ye do what I say" (D&C 82:10). We are told by the prophet Moroni, "that whoso believeth in Christ, doubting nothing, whatsoever he shall ask the Father in the name of Christ it shall be granted him; and this promise is unto all, even unto the ends of the earth" (Mormon 9:21).

We teach our children that God will absolutely and unequivocally answer their prayers, but sometimes we don't believe it for ourselves. This promise is unto *all,* including each of us. As a lawyer, I can tell you that that word "shall" is as direct and final as you can get. It's not "maybe" or "possibly" or "sometimes." It is an absolute mandate. Your Heavenly Father *shall* answer your prayers.

Third, we can have faith that the Lord is in control. The Lord reassured Joseph Smith in a precious revelation, "Thy days are known, and thy years shall not be numbered less; therefore, fear not what man can do, for God shall be with you forever and ever" (D&C 122:9). That reassurance applies to us all. The Lord knows everything about our lives and what will happen to us, and he will be with us through it all. Elder Neal A. Maxwell spoke of this faith, "Faith in God includes faith in His purposes as well as in His timing. We cannot fully accept Him while rejecting His schedule."[6]

My sister has been a good example of this for me. She has been through a lot in her life, but her attitude is amazing. She's always telling me, "The Lord's in charge and everything will work out." Such great faith!

Fourth, we must have faith to hear. This is hard, especially when we're facing scary situations. We are afraid and may or may not want to face that fear, but as we pray with faith, we must be willing to hear what Heavenly Father wants to say to us. Joseph Fielding McConkie has written, "We hear what we train our minds to hear. . . . The revelations of heaven are given in such a manner that all who will hear may hear (D&C 1:11), while those who choose not to hear will not hear (Alma 10:6)."[7] We have to be open to whatever revelation the Lord chooses to give us on these matters.

I remember clearly one situation where I experienced this. I received a phone call from the head of our local Boy Scout Council. I had been very involved in Scouting (four sons, go figure) and was currently serving on the board of directors.

"Merrilee," he said, "we would like you to be the spokesman for the Council. We are in the middle of this lawsuit with the ACLU challenging us on religious grounds and the homosexual issue, and we need someone to deal with the media and speak for us. It will involve local and national media."

I have to tell you, as I was listening, my hands began to shake. In fact, my whole body was shaking. It was crazy! I was really caught off guard by this request. I had absolutely no media training. And taking on the ACLU and the homosexual community was very scary. What would I face? What would my family have to deal with? Could I even do it? Did I even want to do it?

I said a quick but sincere prayer in my heart. I was still shaking when into my head came the clearest voice, "Merrilee, this is your next assignment. You will do just fine." I was startled, but instantly my entire body calmed. I interrupted the executive, who was trying to say anything he could to convince me, and told him I would do it. The rest of the story is amazing and could be the subject of a whole other book. Through the entire experience, I was grateful that in that brief moment, I was willing to hear the Lord. And I was extremely grateful that he answered my prayer, as he always does.

Finally, we must have faith to do. Nephi has this great faith: "I,

Nephi, said unto my father: I will go and do the things which the Lord hath commanded, . . . he shall prepare a way" (1 Nephi 3:7).

President Gordon B. Hinckley shared,

> Who among us can say that he or she has not felt fear? I know of no one who has been entirely spared. Some, of course, experience fear to a greater degree than do others. Some are able to rise above it quickly, but others are trapped and pulled down by it and even driven to defeat. We suffer from the fear of ridicule, the fear of failure, the fear of loneliness, the fear of ignorance. Some fear the present, some the future. Some carry the burden of sin and would give almost anything to unshackle themselves from those burdens but fear to change their lives. Let us recognize that fear comes not of God, but rather that this gnawing, destructive element comes from the adversary of truth and righteousness. Fear is the antithesis of faith. It is corrosive in its effects, even deadly.
>
> "For God hath not given us the spirit of fear; but of power, and of love, and of a sound mind." [2 Timothy 1:7]
>
> These principles are the great antidotes to the fears that rob us of our strength and sometimes knock us down to defeat. They give us power.
>
> What power? The power of the gospel, the power of truth, the power of faith, the power of the priesthood.[8]

At some point, we have to step forward in faith. We must face our fears. We must have absolute faith in the Lord that he will stand by us and help us and prepare a way and that with his help, we can do it. And then we must hold onto our faith, and take that first step.

CHAPTER 4

Women of Peace, Not Worry

I need to warn you, this chapter is a bit dangerous. The tools in it are very powerful. So powerful, in fact, that I received an e-mail from a woman who had heard the lecture I gave on this subject. She wrote, "I love it, I love it. I've used NMP, No Biggie, and more, and it has changed my life. But my kids hate it and have asked me not to attend any more of your lectures. Too bad! I'll be back!"

Women of Worry

I was recently rereading the Mary and Martha story (for the zillionth time) in the scriptures and something new struck me. It was Jesus' comment on Martha's mental state. I always pay attention to Martha because I identify with her so much. Here is what Jesus said: "Martha, Martha, thou art careful and troubled about many things" (Luke 10:41).

I noted this time there was a footnote on "careful" and looked below. And there it was—"worried."

The Savior was concerned for Martha because she was worried and troubled about many things. Not that she was a hyperactive homemaker. Not that she was being judgmental of her sister. Not that she wasn't sitting and listening to him. He was counseling her regarding her tendency to be worried and troubled about so much.

Mary had chosen the Savior. Mary had chosen peace.

I have been a Martha a lot. I spent the first two decades of my life worried and fearful. I was the Worrywart Queen in my youth. I worried about *everything!*

I internalized my worry and my fear so completely that for years I had a severe stomachache. My mother took me to the doctor many times to see if I truly was ill. When I was twelve, my mom got a prescription for "stomach pills" from the doctor. I took one little green pill everyday. And they helped.

And then one day—a day that is clearly etched on my memory—I was walking down the hall past my mother's bedroom and overheard her talking on the phone. "Yes, doctor. The tranquilizers seem to be helping. Her stomachaches have really subsided."

I stood in the hallway in complete shock.

I was on tranquilizers. I was only twelve years old.

I was a mess.

I can remember going into my bedroom and sitting on my bed, still in complete shock. I was overwhelmed with the enormity of my situation. This was before the day when antidepressants were fairly common. Back then tranquilizers were major drugs and taking them was a major deal.

I dropped to my knees and did what I was taught to do in Primary. I prayed. And prayed and prayed and prayed.

"Heavenly Father, I'm a mess. I'm only twelve years old. I shouldn't be on tranquilizers. Help me. Oh, please help me. Teach me how to handle my life."

I learned at a very young age what the phrase "mighty prayer" was all about. I knew that God understood what I was going through. I knew he understood the depth of my worry and fear and that he took it seriously. I could hardly explain what I was feeling to my parents, and I knew they didn't really comprehend what I was experiencing. But I knew Heavenly Father did and that he would help me.

After a long time, I stood up and went and got the little green pills and threw them in the toilet. I told my mother, "I won't be needing the pills anymore."

And so began my tutorial from God. It took many prayers, much fasting, and many years but Heavenly Father literally began to teach a young girl how to cope, and he has taught me well.

I know that many of us identify with Martha. We all have worries and concerns that plague us. Let's face it. I think the minute we were given active hormones, they somehow triggered the "worrywart" gene!

We can begin here together by acknowledging that we often feel we're Women of Worry. In fact, I have developed a worrywart salute so that we may greet each other properly.

With your left hand, form the letter "L" with your thumb and finger. Now do the same with your right hand. Bring the tips of your thumbs together to make a "W." Now take both hands and your giant "W" and smack your forehead three times.

Now I shall greet you: "Welcome Worrywart!" (Please note that I am smacking my forehead.) Now you may respond. Well done!

Welcome to the club! Worrywart Queens unite! You may now salute fellow WW's wherever you meet them. I have to chuckle when I'm walking around BYU campus during Education Week because every once in a while, a woman across the way will give me the Worrywart Salute. I salute back, and we share a great laugh. Of course, other people think we're weird, but they're just jealous.

I shall share with you the motto of the Worrywart Club. I learned this great truth while I was at the physical therapist's office. There it was—wisdom from Corrie ten Boom:

> Worry does not empty tomorrow of its sorrow; it empties today of its strength.[1]

What a powerful statement. I sat and held the framed quote in my hands. I had lived that for years. I had drained the strength out of so many days by worrying.

Another person wrote,

> Worry is fear's extravagance. It extracts interest on trouble before it comes due. It constantly drains the energy God gives us to face daily problems and to fulfill our many responsibilities. It is therefore a sinful waste. A woman who had lived long enough to have learned some important truths about life remarked, "I've had a lot of trouble—most of which never happened!" She had worried about many things that had never occurred, and had come to see the total futility of her anxieties.[2]

And as we have dealt with fear and chosen to be Women of Faith, so too we must deal with worry and choose to be Women of Peace.

Different Levels of Worry

Do you remember the song from many years ago, "Don't Worry, Be Happy"? If only it were that easy! "Don't worry! Be happy!" Right. I'll get right on that.

Does worry affect your life? I would guess that if you have a pulse, you are affected by worry.

Let's delineate worry versus concern. We all have concerns. I'm concerned about my dental care. I'm concerned about whether it will rain today or not. I'm concerned about my finances.

Worry, on the other hand, is concern magnified. It is when the concern is often in your thoughts. You have a problem that you want to fix. Or someone else has a problem and you want to solve it for them. You are worried.

So is normal worry good? Maybe. It's certainly part of living. Every one on the planet worries about something. Worry is not good, however, when it paralyzes you, when it begins to pollute your mind, when it becomes toxic.

That's the next level of worry. Toxic worry is normal worry significantly magnified. This is when you think about something constantly; you can't get it out of your mind. You know your worry is reaching toxic level when you begin to internalize it physically. Our bodies are amazing barometers. They can tell us much if we will only listen.

Where do you physically feel your serious worries? Some may get headaches, even migraines. For others, worry will be carried in their neck or back with recurrent pain. And others will be the stomach-stressers like me. My worries were immediately felt with the grinding gut.

Why Do We Worry?

Why do we worry? I believe the root of worry is the realization that we cannot control externals—other people, circumstances, or events. In addition, we have not mastered the internals—ourselves! Worry is our mind's attempt to deal with these issues.

From *Worry: Controlling It and Using It Wisely,* Dr. Edward M. Hallowell states, "Worry results from a heightened sense of vulnerability in the presence of a diminished sense of power."[3] In other words, worriers either exaggerate the danger they are in, or underestimate or forget about their power to combat it.

What a powerful idea. We exaggerate the danger or underestimate our power. Frankly, I excel at both! (We all have our gifts.)

When I was younger, I hyped up all kinds of things that could happen and ramped up my anxiety to match.

- "Mom's leaving. Kidnappers could come!"
- "Those kids are talking. They're gossiping about me!"
- "We're going skiing. I could die!" (Man, I must have thought I was the worst skier on the planet. It was bizarre!)

Even now I tend to exaggerate things and trigger my worry-wart gene.

- "My friend hasn't called me all month. Maybe she's mad at me!"
- "No one complimented me on my new outfit. Maybe I look totally fat!"

- "No one responded to my e-mail. I just know I've offended the entire Relief Society." (Actually, that may be true. I'm pretty good at unwittingly giving offense sometimes.)

On and on we go, exaggerating the troubles we face. And then we add the twin evil of underestimating our personal power. Recently I was counseling with a woman who was facing a very serious issue. She was grappling with an important ultimatum that she needed to give. I could see the worry ripple across her face.

I asked her a simple question, "Are you strong enough?"

"I don't know!" she fretted, wringing her hands.

I asked her again, "Are you strong enough?"

She looked up at me and looked me in the eye. "Yes, I am. I am strong," she replied with conviction.

"Yes, you are," I assured her. "You are very strong. And you are strong enough to do this."

I received her report the next day that she had walked out of my home, gone home, and delivered the ultimatum. The issue was resolved immediately. I was so proud of her! She had doubted her ability to handle this issue for years. Once she gathered her strength, she was able to resolve it.

I listened to Dr. Barbara De Angelis recently on the radio. Paraphrasing her, she said, "Each of us has the power to make ourselves miserable or we have the power to make ourselves strong. It takes the same amount of energy. So we can choose to make ourselves strong. God gives us all enough personal power. We choose whether we use it to be miserable or to be strong."

It is within our power to choose either to be Women of Worry or Women of Peace. It's up to us.

What Do We Worry About?

We all worry about many things, but there are worries that we all have in common. Luckily, the Worrywart Club has assembled a list. (Aren't you excited to be in a new club? I'm afraid we don't have meetings, however. We're too worried that someone might miss them. ☺)

The Worrywart list includes the following worries:

Money—Do you have any? Do you need more? Are you keeping what you have? Financial well-being is a constant concern of everyone. Even the rich have to concern themselves with managing what they have.

Health/physical—Will you get sick? Are you dealing with health issues already? We all worry about impacts on our health, and we worry about aging. This is a concern that seems to grow over time. My elderly mother and her friends discuss this topic constantly because they are so affected by it.

Relationships—Are you in one? Do you want one? Are the ones you have in good shape? We all worry about our relationships a lot. Because we understand the eternal nature of our relationships—from marriage to children to our eternal nature as brothers and sisters—we have an added level of seriousness to our relationships. There's a lot riding on them!

The unexpected—This can be a tough one. We worry that something might happen out of the blue. I think about this a lot because in my line of work (dealing with administering estates after a death), I get those odd phone calls of, "Fred just dropped dead." I also get calls out of the blue due to my calling as Relief Society president. The unknown and the unexpected are very real worries. Bad things happen, and they can happen unexpectedly!

The future—Oh, to have a crystal ball! What does the future hold? You may wonder, "Will my kids turn out okay?" Or you may worry, "Will I ever get married?" Or you may be concerned, "Will I lose my job?" The future is such a nebulous thing, it could hold some really bad stuff! The less control we have over the future, the worse we feel.

Children—Frankly, I think they give you a "worry card" the minute you give birth. I carry one for each of my children. Some mothers think it's their full-time job to worry and fret about their kids. Surely that's what loving mothers do, isn't it? Who knows what our kids will do? Who knows how they'll turn out? It's scary!

Making mistakes—We also worry about making mistakes. Okay, maybe you don't, but I sure do! I could mess up an estate plan and get sued. I worry about that. You could make a mistake on your tax return. We could make a mistake in public and have people laugh at us. Oh, that's the worst!

Danger—We live in an evil world. No longer do we feel safe. Terrorism, crime, violence—you name it, we're faced with it. There have been two burglaries in our neighborhood recently. Could it happen to us? (I've been tempted to post a sign on my front door to avert this: "Please note, I own no real jewelry except my wedding ring, and I can't pry it off my finger to save my soul. Anything of value has already been broken by my four sons. I don't collect anything except dust. If you're looking for things that are cheap or plastic, please come on in. Feel free to dust while you're here.")

What are your worries? Make your own list. Take a moment to pause and ponder this question. What are you worried about *right now?*

Becoming Women of Peace

I'd like to share with you four phrases to help you become Women of Peace. These are coping mechanisms that will help reduce worry and its effects in our lives.

As we begin, please resist the urge to dismiss these as simplistic. I will give a basic overview on how to use each phrase and principle, but do not underestimate their power—individually and collectively. As you ponder each one and practice using them, you will be surprised at their effectiveness.

As we go over each phrase, check your list and see how many of the worries you've included can be reduced or eliminated by using these coping mechanisms.

Problem Ownership—"NMP"—("Not My Problem")

A big way we get into trouble is falling into what I call the "Martha Syndrome." Like Martha, we are worried and troubled over many things. And most of those things are problems that are not even ours!

I had a visiting teacher many years ago who excelled in this. Here was a typical visit, "Oh, Merrilee, have you heard? Poor Sister Broccoli is getting a divorce. Oh, I haven't been able to sleep since I heard! Isn't that terrible! And have you heard about the Rutabaga twins? Rumor has it they're on drugs. What should we do? I'm just beside myself! And my son, Brussels Sprout, just failed his midterm at college. We're just going to have to deal with that. And oh me, oh my! I heard the elders quorum home teaching is down to 50%. That's tragic. What should we do about it?"

I'm being facetious here, but I am not exaggerating. Practically the entire visit (which amusingly was supposed to address *my* concerns) consisted of her fretting over other people's problems. As a result of living her life this way, she has suffered numerous physical and mental health issues for decades, including depression.

Just as the Lord counseled Martha to release her worries and troubles, he counsels all of us as well. In 2 Nephi 10:23 we are told to "remember that ye are free to act for yourselves." We are taught that everyone has their own ability to choose and that everyone owns the consequences of their choices.

In Helaman 14:30, we read: "And now remember, remember, my brethren, that whosoever perisheth, perisheth unto himself; and whosoever doeth iniquity, doeth it unto himself; for behold, ye are free." I purposely stopped the verse there. Ye are free! Ye are free to make your own choices, and ye are free from owning someone else's choices.

And yet women seem to excel in owning other people's problems. We worry about our children's problems; we worry about our friends' problems; we worry about our spouse's problems; we worry about the entire world's problems!

We often cope with problems by adopting the "happyface." You know how this works. You're standing in church. "How are you, Sister Jones?"

"Why, I'm *fine!*" (You smile broadly.) "Johnny got out of jail this week, and we're all just doing great!" (Keep smiling broadly.)

Or "How is your calling going, Sister Ramirez?"

"Oh, *wonderful!*" (Beaming grin. Do not mention that your last lesson ended with Billy punching Larry and knocking his tooth out and Alisha announcing that she's leaving the Church to move in with her boyfriend. Keep beaming.)

Author Gail Sheehy described "the happyface" so well:

> But it is the average wife and mother, programmed by society to feel responsible for the well-being of those around her, who provides the best clue to why women in general are so fiercely defensive of the happyface. Any speck of discontent on the surface of her own or her family's life is seen as a reflection of a woman's own inadequacy. It must be wiped away. Like waxy buildup, if discontent accumulates, it is her fault—she is a bad emotional housekeeper. And so, because women insist upon shouldering so much responsibility for the way things are turning out in the domestic realm, they must convince themselves that it's all turning out for the best.[4]

"Emotional housekeepers"—I love that phrase! Such an apt description of women! We are practically trained to be "emotional housekeepers" from birth.

Men are judged on whether they have a successful life. Women are judged on whether they have a happy home. So we studiously "manage" the emotional climate in our homes. And it doesn't stop there! We even manage things at work and in our community. It doesn't seem to matter whether we are married, single, with kids, or otherwise. Women just tend to fall into this role of "emotional housekeeper."

So let's practice saying the coping phrase to handle problem ownership: "Not my problem."

Say it out loud. "Not my problem!" Again, with enthusiasm this time! "Not my problem!" Whew, doesn't that feel great! Now you can use the shorthand when time is of the essence. Practice it. "NMP!" Oh, the freedom!

Let's discuss a few situations and practice our new-found phrase.

Your daughter forgets her lunch once again. She is in the sixth grade and will be home in two hours. She calls requesting (didn't I use a nice word there?) that you drop everything and bring her a lunch. What do you say to yourself? Come on—"Not my problem!" Oh, what joy! Then you remind her that taking a lunch to school is her responsibility. What excellent parenting! (And guess what? She will remember next time.)

All right, that felt good. Let's try another.

Your coworker has let his project slide. He was supposed to have the entire PowerPoint presentation done by today. You've already prepared all the handouts as assigned. He comes to you in a panic. "Oh, Jenny. I need you to do this! You're so good at it! It has to be done, and I just don't have time." All together now, "Not my problem!" Okay, you can be a little more diplomatic. Let's try this. "Oh, I'm sorry Justin. I won't be able to do that." (Clench teeth and do not mention that not only has he had three months to get it done, but that you did the presentation the last two times.) Just smile brightly as you stand your ground. Very effective. Throws the other person off completely. How do you respond to someone saying no with a big smile?

You're all doing great! You could also say the "hip" version of "Not my problem." Say it together: "Bummer!" This is a very effective version of NMP and allows you to mix it up a bit. Say it with sadness, hanging your head, "Bummer!" Say it with empathy, furrowing your brow, "Bummer!" You're really getting the hang of this!

Let's practice this version.

Your husband hasn't done his home teaching and wants you to take the phone call from the elders quorum president and cover for him. Let's do it with sadness, "Bummer . . ." (Now, Sister Celery, I saw that. You choked on that one a bit. Try it again.)

Your teenager didn't prepare his talk and comes to you on Sunday morning for a bailout. Let's try empathy this time, "Bummer!" "What!" he says. "Aren't you going to write my talk for me? Do you want me to do a crummy job and have everyone think you're a bad mother?" (Ah, this took great skill. Let's honor it. Once again, with feeling!) "Ah, son, that's truly a bummer!" (This is called the "Double Bummer" and is sometimes necessary with those who try to argue.)

I'll be honest with you, those around you will freak out when you begin to use this phrase. They will be so used to you "helping" and bailing them out and in general owning all of their problems for them that they'll be stunned. You may also need to prepare for backlash as they learn this great tool for themselves.

For example, I was asked if my son would perform in a Christmas program. I committed that he would. (Ach, big boo-boo. I should remember never to make commitments for others!) Luckily, he agreed. "Well, we have to put together a costume," I said.

He replied, "Not my problem. If you don't get a costume together, I'll just stand on the stage buck naked!" Little rat! He had learned this principle a little too well! (Good news, though— we got a costume together in the nick of time.)

I know at this point many of you are thinking, "Oh, I could never say that!" And others are thinking, "Boy, she is a terrible mother!" That's okay. Think what you will. But let's discuss this principle some more.

There is a huge difference between supporting someone and taking responsibility. When we support someone, we allow the other person to fix his or her own problems. When we take responsibility—or "own" their problems—we take over fixing the problem ourselves. Now with respect to children, we must remember that our goal is to raise independent adults, not spineless, perpetual dependents.

It is crucial that we not constantly bail out others or rescue them. They need to develop their own "coping muscles." Many women have their "nurture" mode stuck in hyperdrive and wonder why those around them are weak, lazy, or seem incapable of handling their own lives.

As we consider problem ownership, we also have to remember that there is a scale, say from one to a hundred. For example, your child forgets his lunch on the first day of school in first grade. That may be a time where you don't say "Not my problem," but take the lunch instead.

This actually happened to my last son who called home on his first day. I was stumped. I knew he had walked out with his lunch. Nonetheless, I took one over to him at school.

"Honey, didn't you bring a lunch?" I asked.

"No, Mom. All I had was my morning snack."

And then I realized what had happened. In kindergarten they ate a morning snack, and he thought his lunch was his snack. So from then on we packed him a "Big Eater" bag—a snack *and* a lunch.

So use your judgment in determining where on the scale the issue lies. The best way to do this is to assess the person's ability to solve their own problems. Try to give them some credit. Ask, "Can they deal with this?" If the answer is legitimately yes, back off! Not your problem!

Along the way, we may encounter some sensitive issues. Perhaps you have a family member who is suffering serious emotional difficulty. It would be inappropriate to say, "Gee, honey, bummer!"

Or what about spouses who are less active or not members? What could be the results if we "own" this problem for them? We could resort to nagging, manipulation, criticism, or even ridicule in a desperate attempt to "fix" them. But think for a moment. What if we let *them* own the problem and we merely supported their positive efforts? What if we extended support, persuasion, long-suffering, gentleness, meekness, love unfeigned, and kindness? Ring a bell? (Reread D&C 121.) Perhaps then this spouse would be allowed to work on their spirituality as the Spirit directed them without harassment, albeit well-intentioned, from us.

Another facet of this issue is helping the "needy." There is a fine line between charity and allowing people to learn lessons the Lord wants them to learn by experiencing the natural consequences of their choices and behavior. Here again, the responsibility for the solution must lie with the person involved. Our responsibility extends only to support. If we jump in and solve all their problems for them, then they have not learned.

I once knew a family who had very poor financial management skills. They would overspend significantly, and then ask the bishop of the ward to bail them out. This cycle was repeated over and over. They would get themselves in a financial bind, and then they would go running to the bishop or ward members to help. And the members, in an effort to be charitable, would do so. Everyone would rush in and fix everything. Then within a short period of time, the family would go out and blow the money all over again. After a while, the ward would get a panicky call from the family again.

The bishop realized the family needed to learn financial management skills. He had run into the family in the electronics store where their cart was full of the latest and greatest and most expensive. He knew that as long as they were constantly bailed out, they would never change their ways. They weren't having to feel the pain of the consequences of their behavior.

And so he allowed them to own their problem. And terrible things happened. The family lost their house. They had to rent a house and cut back on their expenses. And they complained bitterly. But after a time of learning to own their own problems, they were able to get control of their spending and buy a new home and do much better with their finances.

Sometimes the most charitable thing we can do is to do nothing. We can love. We can empathize. We can listen. But we do not have to rush to solve other people's problems. Heavenly Father is a very good example for us in this regard. He allows us to work through our problems and issues and he supports and sustains us. But he usually doesn't send down a flock of angels to do the work for us. (Though sometimes I wish he would!)

We have to balance charity with agency and independence. Remember, tremendous growth comes in facing one's problems, and we don't want to deprive anyone of that experience. It doesn't mean we don't love them or support them. It just means that we're not going to drop everything and solve their problems for them.

Sometimes we may choose to nurture and help someone even though it's their problem. We must be sensitive to the Spirit to know when to do so. There have been times when my husband and I were prompted very specifically to bail out a child. And in retrospect we can understand why.

Remember, when we own another's problem, we are saying, in essence, "You can't handle this, so I have to fix it for you."

"Not my problem" gives the message "I have faith that you can solve this." In fact, it's great to say exactly that: "I'm not going to solve this because it's not my problem, but I have complete confidence that you can handle it." What a wonderfully supportive and empowering response!

Of the four phrases we'll cover, this one is certainly the hardest to master. But as you let go and refuse to fix everyone else, they will grow and develop much faster. You will have less of a burden to carry and can, as a result, be *more* of a support to them.

Letting Go

To let go doesn't mean to stop caring; it means I can't do it for someone else.

To let go is not to cut myself off; it is the realization that I can't control another.

To let go is not to enable, but to allow learning from natural consequences.

To let go is to admit powerlessness, which means the outcome is not in my hands.

To let go is not to try to change or blame another; I can only change myself.

To let go is not to care for, but to care about.

To let go is not to fix, but to be supportive.

To let go is not to judge, but to allow another to be a human being.

To let go is not to be in the middle arranging outcomes, but to allow others to effect their own outcomes.

To let go is not to be protective; it is to permit another to face reality.

To let go is not to deny, but to accept.

To let go is not to nag, scold, or argue, but to search out my own shortcomings and to correct them.

To let go is not to adjust everything to my desires, but to take each day as it comes and to cherish the moment.

To let go is not to criticize and regulate anyone, but to try to become what I dream I can be.

To let go is not to regret the past, but to grow and live for the future.

To let go is to fear less and love more.[5]

I love that last line so much: "To let go is to fear less and love more." To me, that means "I love you, and I know you can handle this. I trust you, and I'm not going to be afraid."

As we choose to let those around us own their own problems, we choose peace in our own lives.

It's interesting to see how interwoven guilt is with this principle. Many of us are motivated by feelings of guilt to own others' problems. Perhaps we're the single mother who needs to work full-time. Driven by feelings of guilt over that circumstance, we're up late at night doing our daughter's project for school. Perhaps we feel guilty about the effort we're giving our job, so we take on everyone else's work to compensate. Or maybe we're drowning in guilt that we're not the perfect daughter, so we take on all of our elderly father's problems and race around, trying to manage his life as well as our own.

It's time to toss the guilt! It's time to have less fear. It's time to let our toxic worries go and allow those around us to learn to run their own lives. Surprisingly, once we let this burden go, joy can come back into our lives. We are freed from this load of care with its resentments and emotional toll. As we hand it back, we are suddenly free to offer love—true love—and we are free to feel the joy of that love and the joy of that support. We are free to become Women of Peace.

Perspective—"No Biggie"

The second worry coping phrase is "No biggie." Let's say it together, "No biggie!"

Sometimes our worries come from having a skewed perspective—we're just not seeing things clearly, possibly because of a sense of vulnerability and an exaggeration of danger that we've already discussed. Worries loom over us and appear to be so much bigger and so much more important than they are.

Here are several examples of exaggerated worries that abound:

- "The kids' bedrooms are a disaster. What if someone sees them?" (No biggie: close door.)
- "Oh, I forgot to bake the pie for Enrichment Meeting. I probably shouldn't go." (No biggie: buy one on the way there. Or if you are already there, please note that there a gazillion desserts. I doubt anyone will notice your missing pie.)
- "I can't find it! Now where did I put it?"

Here's a funny example of that last one. My husband misplaced his microcassette recorder. He hunted high and low, and as he did, he got more and more upset. I won't say he was totally berserk but he was approaching it rapidly. He kept coming to me and hoping I would drop everything and help him hunt for it. I helped him look for it for a while, but I was also unsuccessful. I think he wanted me to continue the hunt but the letters "NMP" hung in the air. I think he thought that, in all my perpetual cleaning and straightening, surely I had put it somewhere. Alas, he was mistaken.

Losing things drives my husband absolutely batty, and it was three months before he was finally able to let it go. The following Christmas, he opened up his saxophone case. (He only plays his saxophone at Christmastime.) Sure enough, there it was—his missing tape recorder. We had a good laugh over that one. And yes, he had to eat a bit of crow and acknowledge that I had not "cleaned" it!

Now, whenever my husband starts to fret and worry about a missing or lost item, I'll look at him ever-so-sweetly and say, "Have you checked your saxophone case?" It's my way of reminding him, "Honey, no biggie!"

Some women worry over what their children wear to school. I decided this was not something I needed to fret over. (Having four sons tends to have that effect.) Here's my solution. At the beginning of the school year, I talk to the teacher and say, "In our home, we try to promote independence and capability. So our children select their own clothes and wash them as well. Please be supportive if they don't always look perfectly put-together." So when my boys would show up in clothes that didn't match or looked slept in, the teacher would look at my boy and think, "Oh, isn't that wonderful! He did it all by himself! What great parents he has!" At least, that's what I'm telling myself.

Many years after I began living and preaching "No biggie," I was shopping with my mom. She was talking about all my lecturing. "You know," she said, "one thing you taught me has changed my life. And that's 'No biggie.'" I was surprised. She continued, "I obsessed over everything, and if things didn't turn out just right, I'd be so upset. Now, I just stop my worrying and think, 'No biggie!'"

It has been a wonderful change in my mom. She used to be a perfectionist and would go to great lengths to make sure everything was running perfectly. It's so much better now. Something will happen and we'll think, "Oh, no. Mom's gonna be upset." Then she'll pipe up, "Well, no biggie! Nothing to worry about!" It has brought her (and us!) enormous peace.

Ask yourself, "Will this matter one year from now? Will I even remember?"

When little things happen, we often worry that it means a bigger thing will happen, too, but much of what we worry about never actually comes to pass. It's important to keep our perspective and to keep the little things little. Often we can deflate an emotional escalation with this simple phrase: "No biggie!"

We can also gain better perspective in our lives by remembering our eternal view. I find that when I go to the temple with my list of worries, I walk out with few left. Most fall by the wayside as I focus instead on what we're doing here on earth and what the plan is. All the things that seemed so critical really aren't all that important when I stop to truly evaluate them with a more eternal perspective.

Elder Richard G. Scott has discussed this perspective and priority often.

> In quiet moments when you think about it, you recognize what is critically important in life and what isn't. Be wise and don't let good things crowd out those that are essential.[6]

> When things of the world crowd in, all too often the wrong things take highest priority. Then it is easy to forget the fundamental purpose of life. Satan has a powerful tool to use against good people. It is distraction. He would have good people fill life with "good things" so there is no room for the essential ones. Have you unconsciously been caught in that trap?[7]

Too often we worry about things we perceive as "good" while not realizing that this inflates their importance to the level where essentials are in danger. Our worrying alone can sap us of time and energy to address these priorities. Women of Peace keep their perspective eternal.

One summer, my son Brennan lived in Zambia doing humanitarian work. While he was there, I was fretting over my kitchen remodel, my other son's upcoming wedding, and some lectures I was preparing. Then I received this e-mail from him:

Hello,

Figured I'd give you a quick update on my life in Zambia

currently. I love it here of course and life here is so interesting. Not only do you see horrible conditions everyday and bad living conditions, but even living for me is very humble and farm-like. Our neighbor Mavis has a chicken coop which is fun.

[I'll edit out the next part for you.]

Work on the new children's farm is still progressing. Today we went and cut up a few more trees and loaded up a few truck loads to bring to the charcoal burner. (They bury the logs and cook them to make charcoal.) Then we watered our new banana plants, picked some mangoes, and went to work on the road again. There are lots of petrified trees that make the drive in very interesting. We have to burn tires around the rocks to make them easier to break. Pretty cool how resourceful these people are. It's kind of sad that lots of people are going nowhere just because they have nothing, absolutely nothing, not even good health. Really opens your eyes to how desperate they are to provide and how helpless they can feel. I can't imagine not being able to provide for my family. I don't know what I would do.

Well, life is good and I'm loving it more and more everyday. I love the spirit of the people here and love being around people who are so strong. I love it because now when I talk around them they are saying that I'm starting to talk like a Zambian. :) I love everyone! Well, I need to go get my socks off the clothesline and get tomatoes for dinner so I shall hear from you later!

Something interesting. People there in America complain all the time about gas prices. Let me tell you, in Africa, home to the poorest countries in the world, gas is more then 6 dollars a gallon!! So next time you fill up, feel blessed how CHEAP gas is there. And stop complaining!!! Haha.

That is one thing that I'm sure that will change, NO COMPLAINING. EVER. I am very blessed and very grateful for all the blessings that God has given me. Makes me wonder why I am so privileged; I'm thankful, but shocked how easy life is back home.

Love you all

Brennan

I had to stop and laugh about my stresses. I have a kitchen! Wahoo! And a bed with sheets, blankets, mattress, and a wonderful pillow! And I get to remind Brennan that he can't complain about anything—ever!

I have to admit, since my own trip to Africa, my worries have dropped significantly. It's hard to get all worried and upset over whether my wardrobe is fashionable or whether my son will get an "A" or a "B" on a test. Compared to what I've seen and experienced, a whole lot falls under the category of "No biggie."

Patience—"Hang Loose"

There are many things we worry about that are completely out of our control. And there are other things that literally just take time. For all of these, we must claim patience. So repeat together, "Hang loose."

The Lord has reassured us, "And see that all these things are done in wisdom and order; for it is not requisite that a man should run faster than he has strength" (Mosiah 4:27). I think this applies doubly for women. We do not have to run faster than we have strength. We do not have to handle everything all at once and perfectly. What a relief!

God encourages us to choose patience, "Ye are not able to abide the presence of God now, neither the ministering of angels; wherefore, continue in patience until ye are perfected" (D&C 67:13). "Continue in patience"—that's pretty much good counsel for literally the rest of our lives.

So when do we need patience to alleviate our worry?

- Your son is three years old. All his friends have successfully completed potty training. You can feel the worry and anxiety growing day after day. Stop! Say it out loud. "Hang loose!"
- You have teenagers. Enough said. "Hang loose!"
- You work for a difficult boss. You cannot transfer or quit. Only one choice is left—patience. "Hang loose!"
- Your daughter comes home with brightly colored hair. Luckily, hair can change and grow. Your relationship is in a challenging place already. "Hang loose!"

- Your husband is struggling with work issues. You realize that this is his problem. However, you are dealing with its impact on your home life and marriage. You still feel worry. But choose patience. Choose to be supportive. "Hang loose" as he works through his problems.

Do you worry because results are not available *now?* Again, we can choose patience. We can choose to be Women of Peace.

Peace—"Oh, well"

There are times where it may not be our problem, where we have it in perspective, where we're patiently enduring, and it is still not enough. We have worries left. At this point, we must simply choose peace over worry.

That peaceful submission can best be expressed with "Oh, well." A young woman may express it with more exasperation or resignation, "Whatever!"

The Lord desires that we have this peace in our lives. "Come unto me, all ye that labour and are heavy laden, and I will give you rest. Take my yoke upon you, and learn of me; for I am meek and lowly in heart: and ye shall find rest unto your souls" (Matthew 11:28–29). In John 14:27, he said, "Peace I leave with you, my peace I give unto you: not as the world giveth, give I unto you. Let not your heart be troubled, neither let it be afraid." Such reassurance from the Lord makes clear that he will always be with us.

So when you're vacationing with your family out of state, and you've brought along your property tax bill to pay at the very last minute, and then you *forget* to mail it on time (and thus will incur a very large penalty), realize you have a choice. You can continue to fret and stew about it. Or you can stop worrying and realize that there is nothing that can be done. What's done is done. Time to say, "Oh, well!" and move forward. (Which is what I did. And I never took my bills with me on vacation ever again!) How much better it is to choose peace than have it ruin days or weeks of our lives!

I'm stuck in traffic, and I'm late—"Oh, well." In fact, I was once stuck in traffic, literally rehearsing a speech I was about to deliver on this very topic! I couldn't reach my contact at the venue via cell phone because no one was answering. I could not fly to my destination. As I saw it, I could choose to worry frantically about something completely out of my control, or I could choose to let it go. Well, actually, I *was* getting a little frantic, until I got to this part of the speech and burst out laughing! "Oh, well." I sat in my car saying, "Oh, well! Oh, well!" until it sunk in enough for me to calm down. When I arrived at the venue, I learned they were having a dinner first so I wasn't late after all. Isn't it often like that? I would have worried for nothing and been totally upset by the time I arrived.

You've missed an appointment—"Oh, well!" And yet I have some clients who go on and on, apologizing and feeling terrible. It's done. It's past. Let it go.

When confronted with worries that plague us, we can choose peaceful acceptance. President Gordon B. Hinckley sweetly blessed us with these words, "God bless you, every one, you faithful Latter-day Saints. May there be peace and love in your homes and faith and prayer to guide you in all that you undertake."[8]

Sometimes it's as simple as that. We can simply choose peace. And when our gut starts to twist again, we can stop the cycle and say, "Oh, well." We can release the tension and choose peace.

Give Burden of Worries to Heavenly Father

As I was learning from the Lord how to cope with the worries that beset me, I was led to the Serenity Prayer. As I worked on my new skills, I learned that the ultimate skill is to give the burden of my worries to my Heavenly Father. The Serenity Prayer impacted my life considerably. Every thought taught me what I needed to do. The full version of it is so compelling:

The Serenity Prayer

God grant me the serenity
to accept the things I cannot change;

courage to change the things I can;
and the wisdom to know the difference.
Living one day at a time;
Enjoying one moment at a time;
Accepting hardships as the pathway to peace;
Taking, as He did, this sinful world
as it is, not as I would have it;
Trusting that He will make all things right
if I surrender to His Will;
That I may be reasonably happy in this life
and supremely happy with Him
Forever in the next.
Amen.[9]

This is a truth. We must surrender to God's will, and in so doing, we can find happiness.

Shifting our burdens to the Lord is the final and complete way to achieve peace in our lives. Look up "burden" and "yoke" in the Topical Guide and study them as they relate to the Lord's promises to us.

One of the purposes of the Atonement is to take the burden from us. Christ offers us that gift of peace. But it is up to us to receive it.

The first part is to cast our burden upon the Lord, but the second part is equally important. We must not take it back! Often we pray sincerely and deeply and ask our Heavenly Father to help us, to take away our pain. But then we get up off our knees and take it back! We fret and stew all day over the issue. And then we pray over the same issue that night, asking for the same things.

It's as if we're saying, "I know I asked for help, but I don't think I'm going to get it." Do we have so little faith that we doubt the Lord can handle our burden? He can and he will. Then why do we continue to be filled with such anxiety? Why do we take our burden back?

I cannot answer this. I only know that I do it often.

Once we give the Lord our worry, we have to have faith that his will is what will be done. We must trust in him.

My mother had some wayward children. I watched my mother agonize over them for decades. She prayed; she fasted; and oh, did she fret! It was such an enormously important issue. She desperately wanted her children to be with her for eternity, and so she worried about them continuously.

One day, my mother was praying and having her "wrestle . . . before God" (Enos 1:2). As she prayed, she clearly heard a voice speak to her—the only time it has ever happened in her life. The voice said, "Be still, and know that I am God" (Psalm 46:10). She stopped and looked up. My mother is a woman of tremendous faith. She realized that she did trust the Lord. She did have faith in him. And she would now be still and allow God to not only take her burden from her but also to address the problem. From then on, she didn't take her burden back.

The Lord comforts us,

> Verily I say unto you my friends, fear not, let your hearts be comforted; yea, rejoice evermore, and in everything give thanks;
>
> Waiting patiently on the Lord, for your prayers have entered into the ears of the Lord of Sabaoth, and are recorded with this seal and testament—the Lord hath sworn and decreed that they shall be granted.
>
> Therefore, he giveth this promise unto you, with an immutable covenant that they shall be fulfilled; and all things wherewith you have been afflicted shall work together for your good, and to my name's glory, saith the Lord. (D&C 98:1–3)

Such wonderful reassurance. God keeps his promises!

We can become Women of Peace by remembering problem ownership—"Not my problem"; keeping our perspective—"No biggie"; choosing to be patient—"Hang loose";—and finally, by choosing peace—"Oh, well."

Never forget that Heavenly Father and our Savior, Jesus Christ, love you more than you love yourself. They love your husband, children, sister, or friends even more than you do.

Be still, and know that he is God. And you and I can truly be Women of Peace as we let our worries go.

CHAPTER 5

Women of Obedience, Not Defiance

A woman sat in my living room. She related both her history and her current state of serious disobedience. I asked her, "Who do you want to be?"

"I want to be a good person," she said sincerely. "I want to be a person who keeps the commandments of God." She was a Woman of Defiance who wanted to change her ways and become a Woman of Obedience but was unsure of those first steps.

I thought of this woman, and then reflected on all the things I struggle with—pride, impatience, judging others, failure to do my best—and I realized that I'm a Woman of Defiance in my own way. And like this other woman, I want so much to be a Woman of Obedience instead.

Choosing the Lord's Will

Perhaps "defiance" is too strong of a word. There are many words that can describe our behaviors that are contrary to the will of God: disobedience, rejection, rebellion, noncompliance, ambivalence, you name it!

They all boil down to one thing. A lack of obedience shows

that we are more committed to *our* will being done than we are to the Lord's will being done.

In the book of Moses, the Lord describes this so well when he relates the story of the War in Heaven:

> And I, the Lord God, spake unto Moses, saying: That Satan, whom thou hast commanded in the name of mine Only Begotten, is the same which was from the beginning, and he came before me, saying—Behold, here am *I*, send me, *I* will be thy son, and *I* will redeem all mankind, that one soul shall not be lost, and surely *I* will do it; wherefore give me thine honor. (Moses 4:1; emphasis added)

It is interesting to note Satan's focus. In our family, we like to joke that Satan has "I" problems! His entire focus was on self—*my* will be done.

God continues:

> But, behold, my Beloved Son, which was my Beloved and Chosen from the beginning, said unto me—Father, thy will be done, and the glory be thine forever.
>
> Wherefore, because that Satan rebelled against me, and sought to destroy the agency of man, which I, the Lord God, had given him, and also, that I should give unto him mine own power; by the power of mine Only Begotten, I caused that he should be cast down;
>
> And he became Satan, yea, even the devil, the father of all lies, to deceive and to blind men, and to lead them captive at his will, even as many as would not hearken unto my voice. (Moses 4:2–4)

What a contrast! Christ chose to submit to his Father's will—100%. He chose to be completely obedient.

Letting Go of Our Self

Disobedience and defiance are always motivated by selfishness. We don't want to change. We don't want to give up things. We don't want to work hard. We are motivated by a fixation on self.

It is sometimes hard to admit we do this. We don't want to feel bad about doing bad.

Have you ever had this conversation with one of your children?

"Johnny, why did you hit your sister and make her cry?"

"Well, she started it! She wouldn't pick up the toys like you said we should. So I told her she had to. And, and, and—" Johnny scrambles for some other reason that will justify what he did and make him look better.

As women, one of the things we hate is to look bad. We don't want to look bad physically, and we *really* don't want to look bad socially. We will go through mental gymnastics, trying to justify in our minds why we've chosen to be disobedient. We go to great lengths to avoid facing the consequences and owning up to our choices.

We women not only don't want to look bad to others, but we find it's challenging to even look within ourselves to see these failures. Sins, mistakes, poor choices, disobedience, defiance, rebellion—they're all so difficult and painful to face. And sometimes we go the complete opposite route and live in denial.

I was talking to a woman who obviously had made some seriously wrong decisions in life, but listening to her, you would have thought she was describing picking out cheese! I am no different. When stricken in my conscience by doing something that I shouldn't or by not doing something that I should, I immediately begin to minimize. Honest review is so very painful. And through it all, the self-absorption of the defiant is evident.

One of the ways we attempt to cover or minimize our disobedience is to question the rules.

"But why?" Our kids ask that question a million times until it wears on us like sandpaper, and we do the same.

"But why?"

Following the Prophet

Several years ago I sat in the chapel of our stake center listening to the general Relief Society meeting broadcast. I sat next to a young mom I was trying to encourage to become more active in the Church. We listened intently to President Gordon B. Hinckley:

> We—the First Presidency and the Council of the Twelve—have taken the position, and I quote, that "the Church discourages tattoos. It also discourages the piercing of the body for other than medical purposes, although it takes no position on the minimal piercing of the ears by women for one pair of earrings."[1]

The tension in the room was electric. There it was. A statement from the prophet of God. Clear. Direct. No tattoos. One pair of earrings.

And there I sat with double-pierced ears. I had gotten them for my fortieth birthday. I had fake diamonds in my second set of earrings and thought I looked totally cool! I immediately reached up and pulled them out of my ears.

One of my friends had double-pierced ears as well, but with real diamonds in her earrings. She called me after the meeting. "Merrilee! What did you do about your earrings after the prophet's talk?"

"I took them out and threw them away."

"But why? I don't get it. What's the big deal, anyway?" she questioned.

"It's a question of obedience," I responded.

"Are we expected to be blindly obedient?" she asked. "Can't we know the reason?"

"We don't always know the reasons," I responded. "But I will tell you this. On a personal level, when I got my second set of earrings, I thought I was cool. I was 'hip.' I wasn't quite so old. And when I pulled them out, I realized that I had been excited by worldly things. And I realized that that was a dangerous path for me."

"I just don't think I can do it," she replied. "I love my diamonds, and I think they look great."

"You'll have to decide if your obedience is worth that," I replied.

"Oh, great," she muttered.

It took my friend four months to pull out her double earrings.

She finally realized that she was teaching her daughter that it was okay to be disobedient, and she didn't want to do that. Today she is a bit chagrined to remember that it took her so long to be obedient.

I have to tell you, it was intriguing to watch the various reactions from the women of the Church. Many, of course, didn't have to face the decision as they didn't have extra piercings or tattoos. But many did.

I've heard all kinds of comments:

- "He just doesn't get it. He's old."
- "Why should we have to do something so minor?" (Note to self: read the story of Moses and the brass serpent in the Old Testament.)
- "What's the big deal, anyway?"
- "I don't believe in blind obedience. I'm not pulling mine out until I know why I should have to."

On and on the comments continued. All voices of Women of Defiance. All frightening in their justification of disobedience.

The prophet later repeated his counsel in a talk directed to the youth.

> Respect your bodies. The Lord has described them as temples. . . .
>
> As for the young women, you do not need to drape rings up and down your ears. One modest pair of earrings is sufficient.[2]

Our reactions to such clear and simple direction from the prophet are telling. Are we ready, as women of the Church, for even more direction from the prophet that will be far more difficult to live? If we question and challenge and resist on the small things, will we be ready for what we'll be called upon to face as the last days continue to unfold?

Elder M. Russell Ballard related a wonderful story of a young woman faced with President Hinckley's statement:

> I know a 17-year-old who, just prior to the prophet's talk, had pierced her ears a second time. She came home from the

fireside, took off the second set of earrings, and simply said to her parents, "If President Hinckley says we should only wear one set of earrings, that's good enough for me."

Wearing two pair of earrings may or may not have eternal consequences for this young woman, but her willingness to obey the prophet will. And if she will obey him now, on something relatively simple, how much easier it will be to follow him when greater issues are at stake.

Are we listening, brothers and sisters? Are we hearing the words of the prophet to us as parents, as youth leaders, and as youth? Or are we allowing ourselves . . . to be blinded by pride and stubbornness, which could prevent us from receiving the blessings that come from following the teachings of God's prophet?

Today I make you a promise. It's a simple one, but it is true. If you will listen to the living prophet and the apostles and heed our counsel, you will not go astray.[3]

He identified the twin evils so well—pride and stubbornness! Two faces of that focus on self.

"Just Who I Am"

Not only do we focus on self, but we often focus on the partial, flawed self.

I have a friend who reminds me of this constantly. "I am just who I am!" she'll declare. "I've been a fighter my whole life. I want to be able to say 'yes' or 'no' when I want to. I'm a strong woman. That's just who I am."

She hasn't quite figured out that she can be a strong woman *and* an obedient one.

How often do we hang on to our mortal selves? How often do we buy Satan's lies about ourselves?

- "You can't change; it's just too hard."
- "You were born that way. There's nothing you can do about it."

- "You've been through so much in your life. You shouldn't be expected to do any more."
- "There's nothing wrong with you. God doesn't judge."

That last one always amazes me. Yes, God does judge. He judges with perfect love, and he invites us to obey. He didn't set up his commandments to be guidelines or suggestions with no consequences whatsoever.

Satan is very good at what he does. If he can convince us that we have no need to change or improve, or indeed that we cannot, then he has won a mighty battle. He has stopped our progress just as assuredly as if he had wrapped us in chains. His chains are invisible, however. They are the chains of mortal mediocrity. He has convinced us that our mortal self is our true self. And believing him makes us Women of Defiance. What an awful lie!

And then there are the "gaps." Sheri Dew described this so well when she said, "The mortal experience is filled with gaps: between what we know and what we do; between the ways of God and the ways of man."[4]

Do we have gaps in our own lives? Some of our gaps are large, where we are firmly camped in rebellion, and some of our gaps are small, where we are just short of where we could be. I personally find these gaps really, really annoying. I admit it—they bug me to death.

For example, I know I should have a heart filled with charity. And I do . . . until I see someone who may be different and my heart fills with judgment.

I know I shouldn't lie. And I don't . . . until I need to cover up something.

I know I should be patient. And I am . . . until all four boys are home at once. Trust me. They would try the patience of Job!

These are some of my gaps. I know better. I want to do better, but I don't always do it. And when I don't, I get really frustrated with myself.

Why do I choose to be a Woman of Defiance? Why do I choose to let those gaps exist in my life at all?

I'm not alone in my frustration. A prophet of God, Nephi, shared similar frustrations:

> Behold, my soul delighteth in the things of the Lord; and my heart pondereth continually upon the things which I have seen and heard.
>
> Nevertheless, notwithstanding the great goodness of the Lord, in showing me his great and marvelous works, my heart exclaimeth: O wretched man that I am! Yea, my heart sorroweth because of my flesh; my soul grieveth because of mine iniquities.
>
> I am encompassed about, because of the temptations and the sins which do so easily beset me.
>
> And when I desire to rejoice, my heart groaneth because of my sins; nevertheless, I know in whom I have trusted. (2 Nephi 4:16–19)

I know how Nephi feels! On the one hand, I work hard to be a faithful Saint, and I've had wonderful spiritual experiences and grown a deep testimony. And on the other hand, I'm constantly mired in temptations and sins that plague me. My heart, too, groans, "Merrilee, what are you thinking? You know better!"

Each of us struggles with our shortcomings and the bad or sinful decisions we make. We realize that we know better, but another day comes and on we go, falling short again.

Giving Up Our Sins

My sister has a great tradition. Every New Year's Day, she asks herself this question, "What sins am I hanging on to that are keeping me from God?"

This is a rather interesting question for introspection. Sometimes, to help us cope with our actions, we try to act as if our sins are just accidents. But truthfully, we hang on to them. What sins are we hanging on to? Why? Take a moment to ponder that.

The state of the natural man is very comfy! Living down to the level of our mortal selves is a whole lot easier than having to work at improving ourselves. I am reminded of the television program *What Not to Wear.* On the show, the hosts take people, mostly women, who dress very poorly and teach them how to dress in a more attractive way.

I'm always amused when it comes to the shoes. There are some pretty ugly shoes out there! And every time, the hosts will ask the woman, "Why do you wear such ugly shoes that make you look bad?"

The answer is always the same, "Because they're so *comfortable!*"

"Don't you agree they look terrible?"

"Well, yes, but they're so *comfy!*" And then they go through the painful task of throwing away all the ugly shoes and old clothing. It's so strange to watch these women cling to what they know is bad and unflattering. They hate to give up the familiar and the comfortable, despite the negative consequences.

What ugly old shoes are we hanging on to?

What bits of defiance do we justify and rationalize because they're such comfortable patterns? What areas do we fall short in because it's too far out of our comfort zone to change?

Becoming a Woman of Obedience can be a distinctly uncomfortable experience at first. Are we willing to go through that?

It is also a process that takes time. I received an amusing phone message last week from a frustrated visiting teaching leader. No one had called in their report at the end of the month.

"They should only have to be told once! They know what to do. We coddle the sisters too much!" she declared.

I chuckled over this. Yes, we do indeed know what to do. I know I should exercise more, but alas! The flabby thighs haunt me! We know we should go to the temple frequently and yet, crazy schedules eat away at our time. We know we should study our scriptures faithfully but sadly, we do not.

Obedience takes time. It takes faith. It takes good choices, repeatedly made.

There is a sliding scale from defiant to obedient for choices involving the commandments of God. Every one of us sins, which means that every one of us, to a certain extent, is a Woman of Defiance. But every one of us also makes good and righteous choices, so every one of us is also a Woman of Obedience. We can be in both states of being at the same time. We are always a work in progress.

You may be paying an absolutely perfect tithe but struggle with clean media choices. You may hold perfect family home evenings but struggle with less-than charitable attitudes and behaviors.

So how do we make more righteous choices? How do we more fully become Women of Obedience? How do we invite the joy of faithfulness into our lives?

Our Divine Self

Rather than focusing on our flawed, mortal self, we must focus on our true, spirit selves. Look in your spiritual mirror to see yourself. Then keep a firm picture of your eternal self in your mind. This is who you want to be, indeed this is who you truly are in your core.

Ponder your eternal destiny to get a firm vision in your mind. President Gordon B. Hinckley said, "In a very large measure each of us holds the key to the blessings of the Almighty upon us. If we wish the blessing, we must pay the price. A part of that price lies in being faithful. Faithful to what? Faithful to ourselves, to the very best that is within us."[5]

The Savior offers us the perfect mirror. He was and is perfect. He was the only one born who was able to live a life of perfect obedience. Through his entire mortal journey, Jesus was true to his eternal self. He saw himself clearly and all his choices matched who he saw.

Alma speaks of this view as he encourages us to see and become our true, eternal selves.

> And now behold, I ask of you, my brethren of the church, have ye spiritually been born of God? Have ye received his image

in your countenances? Have ye experienced this mighty change
in your hearts? . . .

I say unto you, can ye look up to God at that day with a
pure heart and clean hands? I say unto you, can you look up,
having the image of God engraven upon your countenances?
(Alma 5:14, 19)

So begin with this clear vision: You are a daughter of God. You
are destined to be a queen. You are of great divine worth. You have
spiritual power and have been saved for these latter days.

One day my sister picked me up from the airport and drove
me down to Provo. We discussed many things. At one point, I
asked her about something related to the Church. She bristled a
bit. I tried to encourage her.

"Well!" she declared. "The Lord will have to accept me just
the way I am!"

I paused for a moment. And then words began to flood my
mind. I turned to her. "Andrea, the Savior *does* accept you for who
you are. He knows you as you *really* are. He sees you as a daughter of God and his sister that he has known for an eternity. He sees
you in white robes of righteousness, a valiant spirit who chose
righteously in the premortal existence, and who has a strong and
indomitable will. He sees you for who you really are. He loves you
for who you really are. *You* are the one who does not know who
you really are."

She was quiet for a long time. The wonderful ending to that
story is that a few years later that sweet sister of mine chose to
turn to the Lord and ask for his help in changing her life. She
attended the temple, and I stood with her in the celestial room. I
saw my sister for the first time actually living as the person she
really was. And she saw herself for the first time as she really was—
a daughter of God, clothed in the beauty of righteousness. Now
Andrea is an amazing, faithful Latter-day Saint woman—a Woman
of Obedience.

Now, we too can commit to live as a righteous daughter of
God. The first step is simple: choose to be a Woman of Obedience.

It Is Our Choice

Sometimes we don't truly make deep commitments. We waffle. "Well, I'll try . . ." "Gee, I'd *like* to . . ."

Instead, take some time to really ponder your commitment. You'll know the difference. There will come a point where you *decide,* completely and totally, to commit to becoming a Woman of Obedience. You'll be able to say, "No matter what, I will be true to my eternal self. No matter what, I will be true to my Heavenly Father and my Savior."

Our family scripture is the clarion call of the prophet Joshua, "Choose you this day whom ye will serve; . . . but as for me and my house, we will serve the Lord" (Joshua 24:15).

The Lord instructs Enoch to declare this same choice to his people, "Choose ye this day, to serve the Lord God who made you" (Moses 6:33).

This does not mean you will never make mistakes or commit sins in the future. It does mean, however, that you are forever committed to facing your mistakes and your sins and doing what it takes to correct them.

Once we are truly committed, it is as Michelangelo said: "I saw the angel in the marble and carved until I set him free."[6]

This commitment extends to all that the Lord asks of us. He truly understands who we really are, and he knows how to help us become who we are destined to be. Our decision to follow him must be absolute. We trust in him fully because we know that he loves us.

This is why Jesus was willing to submit his will entirely to that of his Father. He knew that the Father knew him and loved him and wanted what was best for him. He trusted that knowledge, completely.

Choose to Trust

I think each of us willingly trusts the Savior. We know that the Savior has established his Church to help us grow and become like him, and that he uses mortals to carry out much of the work of his Church. But perhaps for some of us it is a challenge for us to trust his servants.

We may trust the General Authorities, but maybe not our own bishop. We may willingly trust our bishop, but may have real struggles with our Relief Society president. Remember that we are all imperfect beings. We all make mistakes. Our commitment to be Women of Obedience extends to the entire Church. We cannot pick and choose who or what we will obey. The Lord will bless us for our faithful obedience.

Some may argue that this is blind obedience. Some may argue that we should never obey anyone without understanding all the "whys" and "wherefores."

But I believe that there is a place for trusting obedience. When my parents told me not to play in the street when I was young, I did not understand why. I did not have an accurate perception of the danger, but I obeyed in trust.

I trust the prophet. I try to obey him. I do not always do so perfectly. But I do not need to know the reason for every bit of counsel he gives me. I obey him with my eyes wide open.

I trust my stake president. I try to obey him. I do not need to question every policy decision that is made. I accept that his understanding is greater than my own. I obey him with my eyes wide open. I trust in his love for me.

Once we make a deep commitment to be obedient, we then must vigilantly compare our behavior with that goal.

Choose to Repent

Choosing to repent is, at its base, the entire purpose behind daily repentance. It is a daily reflection and review of how our behavior is matching our eternal destiny, which is to become like our Savior. Each day, we can compare where we are that day with the Savior and with our vision of our true self.

Repentance is turning back to our Heavenly Father and the

path that leads us to return to him. It is turning back to being true to our spirit and rejecting the influence of our mortal world.

Daily repentance is most effective. Why? Because it's a lot harder to turn a ship laden with heavy cargo. If, instead, we are in the habit of adjusting our sails and lightening our load every day, it is much easier to stay on course.

Some of us may think, "Gee, I don't really commit a lot of sins every day. This seems to be overkill."

Many of us are very good people. But reflecting daily on how we match up with who we want to be is a necessary and refining process. Think of reviewing your day and looking for ways to improve and be more Christlike as a daily refinement that will bring you closer to Christ.

When we express sorrow and regret over our "gaps," Heavenly Father can then begin to teach us how to close them. If we don't stop to look at them and feel bad about them, we stop our growth. Meanwhile the Lord patiently waits for us, encouraging us, "You could be so much more!"

Repentance can be a joyous process. We can face the guilt of sin, commit to a righteous life, and catch the joy of the Atonement. The Atonement does not have to be for major sins alone. We can feel the joy of the cleansing power of the Atonement each and every day for all the small imperfections that beset us. Each day, we can feast on the fruit of God's love. That joy can be exquisite.

Women of Obedience also acknowledge the companion choice of the choice to be obedient: The choice to repent regularly and sincerely. They know this is a crucial step to growth. They know that daily turning and returning to the Savior is the surest path to returning home.

After making the commitment and reflecting daily on our progress, we have to build our own foundation of living a life of obedience.

The Basics

We all know what we should do. I've taught for many years, and I still crack up over the "pat" answer. Each week, a teacher will ask, "What should we do to (fill in the blank) in our lives?"

Bam. Up goes the hand. "We should pray and study our scriptures."

"Yes, yes, but what else?" the teacher probes.

It's the same everywhere.

When will we stop thinking the pat answer is the end and recognize that it is, instead, the beginning?

So let's start there. With the pat answers.

"Do I pray daily and have sincere and deep communion with my Heavenly Father?"

Well. Sort of. I say my prayers.

That phrase strikes me: "I say my prayers." Yes, many of us faithfully "say" our prayers. But do we *pray*? Do we commune with our Heavenly Father? Do we communicate with him on a sincere and personal level? Or do we rattle off the same things and the same phrases day after day?

If we are to survive spiritually, we have to constantly reinforce and improve our spiritual habits, and none is more important and basic than daily prayer.

A question I ask myself is, "Has the quality of my prayers improved in the last few years?" Sometimes that is a painful question to ask. I, like you, am a very busy person. I struggle sometimes with the commitment to place my relationship with my Heavenly Father first in my life—both in time and in intensity.

Second question: "Do I study my scriptures with the Spirit?"

Well. Sort of. I read them pretty often.

Again, there is a big difference between simply reading a few verses and studying with the Spirit.

How is my study of the word of God? Do I casually read bits and pieces, just to check it off my list? Is it a spiritual habit of mine, or something I add to my list from time to time?

And how many times do I gloss over those answers, and ask, "Anything else?"

One year, this struck me forcefully as I was reading.

I asked myself, "Why do I keep asking what *else* I should be doing, when I need to work on the basics?"

The Perfect Year

I'd like to share with you a powerful experience that has changed my life and the commitment I give to spiritual habits. Before I do, though, I want you to remember that the most important thing we can do when praying and reading our scriptures is to draw close to our Savior and internalize the truths we receive and try not to do these things simply to check them off our list.

As I pondered the basics I might incorporate into my life, I decided to begin at the bottom. I wanted these two spiritual habits—prayer and scripture study—to be absolutely dried-in-concrete habits in my life. I didn't want it to be hit or miss anymore. I didn't want to listen to yet another Church lesson and think, "Yep, I should do better at reading my scriptures," and once again start 1 Nephi with intentions to make it all the way to 2 Nephi this time but then never make it there.

What if I committed to living just these two spiritual practices perfectly?

Then, a bold thought took hold in my brain.

Perfectly. As in every single day. As in nothing missing.

And so the idea of the "Perfect Year" was born. I committed right there that I would live a perfect year of daily prayer and scripture study. I decided that I would establish a minimum behavior: prayer twice a day and reading at least one verse from my scriptures. I had to actually *open* my scriptures to read or actually listen to the scriptures either on CD or on my computer—just reciting one to myself wouldn't count!

Now you may say, "Gee, Merrilee. Why didn't you commit to

reading a whole chapter? Or half an hour a day? One verse seems a little chintzy."

That may be true, but my goal was not necessarily to read the scriptures during a set time or to finish them in some kind of deadline—my goal was to be successful in developing a *daily habit* of reading the scriptures, and I knew that some days would be incredibly challenging. I also knew that if I focused all my effort on opening my scriptures to read at least one verse, I would likely read more. But if my goal was to read for a half hour, I'd constantly put it off all day, trying to find a clear half hour in my schedule, which, to be realistic, I knew would rarely come.

Part of my goal was to develop and increase my love for the scriptures. I figured it followed that if I loved the scriptures more, I'd read them more, right? And being motivated by love is much more effective than being motivated by guilt, as we've discussed.

I set a rule for myself that if I missed a day, I would start my perfect year again, and that would be okay. If I had to start again in August, it was still good. I would be working on a wonderful thing and would simply begin again! No guilt allowed!

I had this experience at the end of April, so I made a commitment that May 1 would be the day that I would begin my perfect year.

The first week went easily, and I read far more than one verse each day, happily.

The second week went okay.

By the third week, I had to really persevere. There were some crazy days! I prayed for help. After a month of daily reading, I didn't want to waste all my efforts! So, I kept plugging away at it, day after day, week after week.

Yes, some days it was 11:52 AM, and I'd suddenly realize I had forgotten to pray that morning. I'd stop everything, leave the meeting, and go out to my car to pray. And oh, yes, there were nights when it was 11:52 PM, and I'd whip open my scriptures and read aloud a verse or two to my husband.

I went to Africa during my Perfect Year and that was a

challenge! I skipped a day crossing all the time zones and I couldn't figure it out so I read and prayed a lot just in case! (I know, I know. Shades of obsessive-compulsive disorder, but it's better to be safe than sorry.)

I remember one night so clearly. I was in Zimbabwe, staying in a Church member's home. I was absolutely exhausted from the emotional strain of the humanitarian work we were doing and from the new and different experience of being in Africa. It was October. I had had a perfect year since May 1.

I fell asleep.

In the night, I woke up with a start. What was it? Had I heard something? (It was rather nerve-wracking to be told to stay behind the hall door while they set the laser alarm system so we'd be safe at night.) And then I heard the Spirit softly whisper, "Merrilee, you forgot to read your scriptures." I turned on the light and saw that it was 11:45 PM! And yes, I read my one verse, and then I uttered a long prayer of gratitude, thanking Heavenly Father for helping me reach all my goals.

I completed my perfect year 365 days after I began. It was nothing short of miraculous. I had focused an enormous effort on these two spiritual habits and, with tremendous help and reminders more than once from the Spirit, it worked.

I continue those habits even now. I have missed a day since, much to my agony, but I decided that was a good exercise in humility. (At least that's my story, and I'm sticking to it.)

I cannot begin to tell you of the difference that building those habits has made in my life and in the lives of my family. It has been tremendous. I cannot let a day pass, now, without feasting on the word. Some days it is a moment as I savor one verse, and it will linger with me and touch me all day. Some days it is an hour of deep prayer and study. Each day is different, but no day is empty.

I have to admit that it feels so good not to feel guilty! And oh, the joy! How can I share with you the joy? To have the Spirit be a force in my life every single day—the joy is incredible.

I'd like to share a funny experience I had last fall after this had become a habit. We live in Southern California, and once again our city was ravaged by wildfires. I had been working at the evacuation center all day and came home very late. I was in my office, chatting with my sister and brother-in-law who had been evacuated from their home. Just that day, they had found out that their house had not burned though many of their neighbors' homes had. We were grateful that both of our homes were safe.

We began discussing the Holiday Boutique that my sister was going to organize for the fire victims. (A second time, I might add. She had held one four years prior after the last terrible round of wildfires.)

We were chatting some more when I stopped suddenly, "Wait! I have to read my scriptures!"

My sister laughed. "Well, read it out loud so we can all count it," she said.

I grabbed a little paperback Book of Mormon and whipped it open. I had to hold it waaaay back because I hadn't grabbed my reading glasses. I peered down and read, "And Alma said: Be it according to the will of the Lord. But, behold, our work is not finished; therefore they burn us not" (Alma 14:13).

We just bugged out our eyes. And then we burst out laughing.

"That's it!" I cried. "Our work is not finished because we didn't burn!"

We laughed and laughed.

There have been countless other times when I have read a verse that suited my situation perfectly. I have realized that even if I had to restart my "perfect year" many times, it has been worth the effort. All the good improvement we make is still good, even if it's not done perfectly. We have still done something good for ourselves that has improved our lives, mistakes and all.

Since my first perfect year, I applied that powerful principle to other behaviors. I have discovered the sheer focused effort on improvement is worth it.

Often women approach me and ask how I accomplish as much as I do. I joke that I gave up cooking and it has saved a lot of time!

But then I honestly say, "I try every day to put first things first. Prayer and scriptures. After that, the rest fits in much better." I think we kind of hope there could be something else to it. But spiritual power is not complicated, and when we have that spiritual power in our lives, we can take care of the temporal stuff a lot easier. Gaining that spiritual power is simple. It just takes consistent effort.

Obedience with Exactness

One of the concepts I ponder when contemplating how to become a Woman of Obedience is how to have obedience with exactness in my life. I've heard many people use that phrase and it's something I've given considerable thought.

I love the story of Nephi, the prophet alive when Christ came to America after his resurrection. Nephi endures a big personal and political uproar when he accurately prophesies of the death of the chief judge. Then, as he is walking home thinking about what has happened, the voice of the Lord comes to him and gives him the power to seal. The Lord commands him to go preach repentance. Nephi has had quite a full day! A lot has happened! He dealt with a mob, was arrested, was released, and then received a powerful revelation. (It makes my busiest day look a little drab!)

But now he receives this commandment to go preach, and he knows the people are not going like what he has to say. What does Nephi do?

> And behold, now it came to pass that when the Lord had spoken these words unto Nephi, he did stop and did not go unto his own house, but did return unto the multitudes who were scattered about upon the face of the land, and began to declare unto them the word of the Lord which had been spoken unto him, concerning their destruction if they did not repent. (Helaman 10:12)

Nephi turned on the head of a dime! He didn't wait until the next day. He didn't take a nap first. He didn't calculate how he could make the message more politically correct so that he wouldn't offend anyone. He immediately stopped, turned, and did the will of the Lord. I've always been impressed by Nephi's obedience with exactness.

The children of Israel often struggled with this concept, but at one point they were willing to obey. They told Moses, "Go thou near, and hear all that the Lord our God shall say: and speak thou unto us all that the Lord our God shall speak unto thee; and we will hear it, and do it" (Deuteronomy 5:27).

Simple obedience: "We will hear it, and do it."

Obedience with exactness is a struggle because of the pull of the world.

Peter understood this struggle well. And yet, he also understood clearly the choice he faced. When accosted by the officers of the temple, he responded: "We ought to obey God rather than men" (Acts 5:29).

It is clear. But it is not always easy.

Our obedience can improve, and even the quality of our obedience can grow. We just need to be aware, humble, and willing.

Finally, we must search out our motivation behind our obedience. This is crucial. We must pass the Pharisee test.

The Pharisee Test

A couple of years ago I read a fictional series about the life of Christ. Many people had raved about this series and told me how much they had grown in their love for the Savior. I did as well, but what really struck me in my reading was the character who was a Pharisee. I found him to be fascinating. I read with interest as this Pharisee—who was a pious and seemingly extremely righteous man—was confronted with Jesus' constant condemnation of the Pharisees.

He didn't get it. Wasn't he reading the scriptures more than anybody? Didn't he obey all the commandments with far more exactness than anyone else? Didn't he attend synagogue more than anyone and didn't he hold a really important calling? He was baffled by Christ's vehement condemnation of those who were esteemed so highly by everyone else.

The transformation of this Pharisee begins as he is led to confront the motivations behind his obedience. He realizes, to his shame, that virtually his entire motivation is selfish. It was a painful realization. It was also a humbling one. And it was at that point that the Pharisee's heart opened, and he began to truly learn.

I found myself thinking of him over and over again. One day I was standing in my kitchen, and I thought to myself, *Christ consistently condemned the Pharisees. Okay, so who would be a Pharisee today?* I instantly thought of a man I know. He is absolutely devoted to the Church. He loves having "big" callings. And he is a lousy husband and father. I thought, *Oh yeah, he is really a Pharisee.*

And then I experienced almost a physical jolt as within a second of having that thought, it hit me—*I* was a Pharisee! And frankly, if I had lived in Jesus' time, I would have been a really *good* Pharisee!

How many times had I taken pride in having a "big" calling? How often had I been so happy when I could whip out a scripture reference in class and impress everyone? How many times had I compared myself to others and judged them harshly? How often was I proud of my righteousness? How much of my obedience had been motivated by pride?

I have to tell you, it was staggering to realize how much. I was absolutely smitten to my core. I stood in my kitchen and wept.

Then the Spirit whispered, "Good, now we can begin. Now you can learn."

I clung to that. Oh, how I wanted to learn! It was not enough to be strictly obedient. I needed to be pure in my heart.

I will admit that it was a very painful year of learning. In fact, my learning continues to this day. I often think of something I've said or done and pondered the question, "Now what is my motivation?" Over and over.

The Spirit has been working to teach me, though at times it has felt like the pounding and molding would break me. It is startling to be this old and realize that you have to go back to square one!

The Power of Love

One lesson I have learned is this: perfect obedience is motivated by *love*. That's it, pure and simple.

When my obedience is motivated by love, I don't feel it necessary to compare myself to others. It's hard to explain, but now, when I see people who are at a different point on the path of life, I don't look at where I am and measure the difference. I am filled with love for them for where they are and the progress they have made. And I want to help them along their path. Not so that they can "catch up to me." They might be ahead of me. The different points are irrelevant. Also, when I am motivated by love, I can look at someone who may be more spiritually developed than I am and not feel either jealous or inadequate. All the comparisons of obedience become irrelevant in the face of love.

Christ's motivation for obedience to the Father has always been love. We can choose to have our obedience be motivated by the same thing. It takes reflection and evaluation to delve into our motivations, but as we do so, the Lord will work with us and help us.

Women of Obedience are guided by love, and as we stretch our hearts to increase that love, our behavior naturally follows.

One day I was on my prayer/walk and all of a sudden, I thought of something I had done and realized, to my horror, that it was dishonest. I had not seen it clearly before. I felt terrible.

And then I realized that because of my dishonest action, for which I now had a great desire to repent, Christ had to suffer. Oh, I cannot tell you how I felt then. I had caused my Savior to suffer for something I had done. I began to weep uncontrollably. The thought of his suffering because of me caused me unbearable pain. I love him so dearly! How could I ever have done such a thing?

I repented probably more sincerely than I have ever done in my life. I repented of causing him pain.

I wasn't sure I could go on. How could I even function? What if I did something else—which I surely would do? I stood stock-still.

And then his sweet assurance came. I was filled with the knowledge that he loved me enough that he was willing to suffer for every single thing I had done and would do. He loved me. Truly.

All he asked was that I would try. Each day. Try to be more obedient, and when I messed up, to turn to him, repent, and try again.

I do not understand the depths of that love. But I know it is real.

And now we, as Women of Obedience, do

> witness unto thee, O God, the Eternal Father, that [we] are willing to take upon [us] the name of thy Son, and always remember him and keep his commandments which he has given [us]; that [we] may always have his Spirit to be with [us]. (D&C 20:77)

We so witness because we love our Savior. When faced with decisions, we covenant to remember his love for us, and we feel profound joy in that love.

CHAPTER 6

Women of Strength,
Not Weakness

I had borne my testimony that day. And I was a weeping mess by the time I was done, which is pretty normal for me. A man came up to me after the meeting.

"I was sure surprised that you are such a softie," he commented. "You seem like such a strong woman and yet there you were, crying like a baby. I didn't expect that."

Thanks eversomuch.

A strong woman. What does that mean?

Obviously to this man, it included the ability to repress one's emotions. I suppose it was reflective of his cultural conditioning, "Strong boys don't cry. Now stop."

Woman of Strength. What does it take to be a woman of strength? Do we have to reinvent ourselves or contort our personalities to fit the "strong woman" mold?

I would say I am a Woman of Strength in most ways. As I've mentioned in previous chapters, this strength was hard-won. And yet, I still have weaknesses "which do so easily beset me" (2 Nephi 4:18). What do I do with them? Do I have to eliminate them in order to keep my "strong woman" card, or do I just have to hide them really well?

This topic is near and dear to my heart because I had a rather shaky, weak start in life. As I've mentioned, I was filled with fear and worry and battled depression for many years throughout my youth. I felt like a walking mass of weakness, and it was only through struggling with those issues and turning those weaknesses into strengths that I was able to progress and develop as a woman.

Now frankly, all of us begin our lives with weakness. It's called being children. But we have progressed in many ways, so we understand a great deal how this process works. As we overcome the weaknesses of fear and worry, we find they lead to strengths of assertiveness, faith, and confidence.

The theme of becoming strong Saints has been emphasized by President Gordon B. Hinckley. He said: "The time has come for us to stand a little taller, to lift our eyes and stretch our minds to a greater comprehension and understanding of the grand millennial mission of this The Church of Jesus Christ of Latter-day Saints. This is a season to be strong."[1]

President Hinckley repeatedly admonished us that we need to be strong. It is a time when it is not enough just to be honorable, but we must be valiant in our testimonies of Jesus Christ and in our behavior as Saints of God. And so it is crucial for us to develop this spiritual strength in our lives, and it will certainly be crucial in the lives of our children.

I grew up during the "Women's Movement" and was very affected by the dramatic shift in the cultural view of women. Parts of this movement were very damaging. I had a hard time looking forward to wifehood and motherhood because those roles had been so denigrated during my youth. Other parts of this movement were very invigorating. I truly believed that I could be anything and do anything. That was indeed liberating!

However, I was offered a view through a rather distorted lens. In stark contrast, I was taught that women of strength were those who had active careers and endless capabilities while women of weakness were those who were stay-at-home homemakers with cloudy goals for the future.

Thankfully, the truths of the gospel of Jesus Christ offered a clear lens. Being a woman in the gospel is the ultimate path to becoming a Woman of Strength. The roles of woman, wife, mother, and sister are elevated and revered in an eternal perspective. The vision of our eternal destiny as a queen trumps any attraction to worldly accomplishments.

But we are women living in the world. And the world has definite opinions about us and our roles. We also live in a Church culture that is rather unique, in and of itself, with forces and opinions of its own.

We all began as girls born into families that have their own opinions on women. Many of us were given dolls to play with and roles to emulate. We were taught many things as we grew. The training we received as girls and women had some wonderful results, helping us to prepare for our eternal roles as wife and mother. So many women in the kingdom are loving, sweet, and kind. Many nonmembers I meet comment on how wonderful Mormon women are, how giving and caring they are. And I believe these comments are well justified.

But this training also can have a negative impact on women's personalities. I call this the "Doormat Syndrome."

The Doormat Syndrome

We are taught and trained that our husbands are to be the head of the home. The priesthood leads in the Church. Mothers with young children are to be in the home. We are taught to be obedient, meek, and humble. These are good principles and virtues and, frankly, they are essential to our eternal success. But some of us take this view too far and become so subservient and weak that we become "doormats." You've seen this, and perhaps you've even experienced this.

Add to this the tremendous burden that Mormon women carry. Our actions as women and mothers are eternally significant. As Latter-day Saint sisters, we are not just trying to raise children, we're preparing Saints for eternal exaltation. If our marriages or our children don't turn out perfectly, we feel tremendous guilt that goes way beyond that experienced by non-LDS women who don't feel the weight of eternity on their shoulders. Add to this the chaos that is normal in a busy Mormon household and it can be a volatile mixture.

What makes this all so difficult to deal with is that we often don't have the training that we need to meet these challenges. We excelled in our classes at Mormon Woman University—got an A in Humility 101, high honors in Obedience 104, top of the class in Contentment 203. But these attributes alone don't always address the behavior and skills we need to deal with the tasks we are given. Sometimes we aren't naturally Women of Strength.

I saw this in great clarity several years ago in my own stake. I was the area coordinator for the Marriage Initiative that was on the ballot in California. The initiative was in favor of traditional marriage, and the Church supported this measure. My task was to develop a team of volunteers who would contact all the households in a large area and encourage voters to vote in support of the proposition.

We began this process by holding many home meetings where we discussed the initiative and then tried to recruit volunteers to sign up to go door-to-door. I began by contacting people I knew from throughout my stake, and I was stunned at the reaction.

The first meeting really opened my eyes. Every woman in the room declined to participate. The comments were very similar.

- "I could never do that!"
- "I'm terrified of talking to other people."
- "My husband can do it for our family."
- "What would people think?"

Most of these women were middle-aged or older. I could not believe what I was hearing, and I walked out of that meeting shaking my head. I commented to the bishop who was walking next to me, "I would hate to be that afraid of people in my 50s."

Not one woman in that room felt she was equipped with the

assertiveness, the skills, or the *courage* necessary to defend her testimony of the eternal family and the plan of salvation.

Now as this process of recruitment went on, we did find some women who were able to stand up and help, but it was sad to see the large proportion of women who did not. I thought, *We ask our nineteen-year-old missionaries to do far scarier things than this!* So, what was the difference between the women who couldn't help and the women who could?

I suspect that somewhere along their path, those women who chose to participate had learned and acquired the strength they needed to do what needed to be done. But many of the other women had not. So where can we get this strength? As I have said, many of us were highly trained in the "womanly ways"—attentiveness, nurturing, and intuition, among others—and frankly, those womanly ways come pretty naturally to most of us. What does not seem to come naturally to some is strength. But it can be learned.

Some of us learn it the hard way. We experience great trials in our lives—perhaps ill health, death of a loved one, or divorce—and we develop great strength as we cope with these things. I think of my friend Sue, who has experienced several of these trials. She is a woman with a core of steel. She has *earned* her strength.

But do we all have to experience tragedy before we can develop strength? I don't think so. I can learn from my other sisters' experiences as they share with me the things they've learned along the way without my having to experience the same difficult events. Developing strength does not have to involve trials and suffering.

Turning weakness into strength is necessary if we are to become Women of Strength, fit to serve in the kingdom of God.

But first, it may be helpful to get a handle on what our weaknesses are and how we define them.

Weakness Defined

If I were to describe to you a very small, very poor woman who spent her entire life in an impoverished third-world country, would you think "strong" or "weak"? What if I added that she had no formal education and never held a paying position in her life? By now, you would most assuredly think "weak." Let me finish by telling you her name—Mother Teresa of Calcutta. This humble woman was revered by powerful leaders of the world and loved by millions. She won the Nobel Peace Prize in 1979 for her dedication and efforts.

So, as we list our weaknesses, can we toss out small of stature and poor? Also, can we throw out lack of education and high-paying career while we're at it? All of these supposed weaknesses were irrelevant to Mother Teresa's strength.

Let's consider another woman. Born in Russia, she emigrated to the United States as a child. She married and became a school-teacher in Wisconsin. Your perception? Wife, mother, teacher. Nice lady. But maybe not necessarily a paragon of strength. Then she and her husband felt the call of Zionism and moved to what was then Palestine, where they raised two children. She felt inspired to help the women in her country, so she began to be involved in many civic groups.

Okay, so she did some volunteer work, too. Sounds sweet, though still not necessarily strong. Let's add her name: Golda Meir. She was one of the founders of the state of Israel and became its first female prime minister. She met with many world leaders to promote her vision of peace.

It has been said of her,

> Dates and positions do not begin to explain the lasting positive influence of Golda Meir. She is still deeply loved today by her people and by millions more throughout the world. Her dedication to her country and her personal concern for all people are legendary. Whatever Golda Meir did, she did for the people.
>
> If Greatness is given a name, it surely is Golda Meir.[2]

So if we are listing weakness, let's also throw out lack of social status, immigrant, and motherhood.

Our next woman was born in Alabama and suffered a

debilitating illness as a small child. She never married and never had children. She could not speak well.

Maybe at this point, you're looking for a word that goes beyond just *weak*.

Let me tell you the end of her story and see if you can fill in the middle. She was a world-famous speaker and author, writing many books. She was very involved in political and social causes and is remembered as a great advocate for people with disabilities. She received the Presidential Medal of Freedom, one of the United States' two highest civilian honors. She was listed on Gallup's Most Widely Admired People of the 20th Century and was featured on the state quarter of Alabama. Can you guess who she was?

Let's fill in the middle. She was the first deaf and blind person to ever graduate from college. Yes—Helen Keller.

Now we can also throw out marital status or lack of mortal motherhood as weaknesses. We can also throw out disabilities, including severe and multiple handicaps. We can toss the ability to speak well.

Goodness gracious! What do we have left?

What *is* weakness?

Is it when you're quiet and reserved? I would argue not. Volume alone does not equal strength. Some of the loudest women I know are dealing with major, debilitating weaknesses. My friend Kate is a very bold, opinionated woman. And yet she is extremely sensitive and gets offended very easily.

Is it when you're shy? I'm not sure on this one either. Many great artists and poets have been described as shy and struggled with it their whole lives.

I guess if I were to describe weakness I would call it "limiting behaviors or attitudes."

A woman gripped by fear is weak. Why? Because this attribute and its resulting behavior is limiting. A fearful woman will have difficulty rising to her potential.

A woman who constantly feels guilt as she compares herself with worldly standards and with others is weak. Why? Because she has set her standards at a lowly mortal standard and is comparing herself to faulty façades alone, both of which will limit her ability to grow and develop.

Each of the women I described—Mother Teresa, Golda Meir, Helen Keller—was able to work past her limitations in truly remarkable ways. None of them allowed her perceived weaknesses to stop her progress and development. Each was able to transcend the cultural restrictions that she faced and rise above them to have an amazing life of leadership and influence. Each became a Women of Strength in her own right.

President Monson spoke of the strength that comes from self-mastery.

> The battle for self-mastery may leave a person a bit bruised and battered, but always a better man or woman. Self-mastery is a rigorous process at best; too many of us want it to be effortless and painless.
>
> Instead of making an effort, some people make excuses for not doing what they could be doing. We hear the argument, "I was denied the advantages others had in their youth." Others say, "I am physically handicapped." But history is full of examples of people with physical handicaps who went on to greatness. The Greek poet Homer, the English poet John Milton, and the American historian William Prescott, had good excuses—they were blind. Athenian Demosthenes, greatest of all great orators, had a wonderful excuse—his lungs were weak, his voice was hoarse and unmusical, and he stuttered. The great German composer Ludwig van Beethoven continued to compose even after he became totally deaf. They all had good excuses for not doing anything—but they never used those excuses.[3]

God Knows Our Weaknesses and Our Strengths

Weaknesses in ourselves can best be discovered through constant prayer and reflection. This is important because God alone understands our true weaknesses.

The world may look at a mother working full-time and full-tilt and see a woman of success. But God understands the heart of this woman and can see what may be her weakness of worldliness and selfishness that others do not. Or God may understand the heart of this woman and see her sincere love for her family and the unknown circumstances that require her to be in this position. God alone knows what is in her heart.

We cannot rely solely on the perceptions of others to detect our own weaknesses because other people's perceptions of us are often incomplete or flawed. It would be ridiculous to feel bad about some of our attributes solely because others have criticized us for them. I have a friend who is mostly deaf. Others have criticized her for speaking softly and for struggling with her new calling. Can you imagine? I think it is outrageous that they criticize her, not knowing all the facts. And it would also be downright silly for her to "buy into" their criticisms.

I have another friend who, lately, has been less than organized in meeting the requirements of her Church assignment. Many people have been critical of her. Little do they know that she is working three jobs to help keep her family afloat and is exhausted much of the time. I think it's crazy that others would criticize her, not knowing all the facts. And again, it would also be ridiculous for her to agree with their assessment of her.

We must not hand our personal power to others, to allow them to assess whether we are weak or strong. Other people have absolutely no idea.

Instead, we must turn to our Heavenly Father who will reveal to us our weaknesses and areas needing improvement.

As I mentioned previously, I took great pride in my righteousness. It took a conversation with my Heavenly Father to realize that this was actually a serious weakness that needed correction. If I had strictly relied on the assessment of others, I would have remained weak—hampered by my pride—and I would not have understood my failure to progress in spiritual strength.

Elder Dallin H. Oaks spoke on the topic of our strengths

becoming weaknesses in his great talk, "Our Strengths Can Become Our Downfall":

> We generally think of Satan attacking us at our weakest spot. . . .
>
> But weakness is not our only vulnerability. Satan can also attack us where we think we are strong—in the very areas where we are proud of our strengths. He will approach us through the greatest talents and spiritual gifts we possess. If we are not wary, Satan can cause our spiritual downfall by corrupting us through our strengths as well as by exploiting our weaknesses.[4]

It is only by turning to our Heavenly Father that we can truly identify our weaknesses and vulnerabilities that need attention as well as our strengths that may need "adjustment" before they damage our souls.

The Lord encourages this process of identifying weaknesses and strengths. Mormon was concerned that his writing was weak and wouldn't convey the necessary spiritual power. The Lord explained to him in Ether 12:27, "And if men come unto me I will show unto them their weakness. I give unto men weakness that they may be humble; and my grace is sufficient for all men that humble themselves before me; for if they humble themselves before me, and have faith in me, then will I make weak things become strong unto them."

As we examine each of the elements of this verse, a formula emerges for transforming weakness into strength. It provides many keys to becoming Women of Strength. I call this the "Prophet Formula."

The Prophet Formula: Transforming Weakness to Strength

1. Recognize your weakness. The scripture says, "if men come unto me I will show unto them their weakness." So the first step is to turn to the Lord to get a more complete understanding of what weaknesses we have that need strengthening. This will take time. Most of all, it will take a willing openness. It can be a painful process to have the Lord point out our weak areas. But if we aren't willing to look, he can't help us. When we are willing to accept the corrections of a loving Savior, true progress can be made in this crucial first step.

2. **Become humble before God.** "I give unto men weakness that they may be humble." This is the very purpose of our weaknesses—so we can become humble before our Savior, so we will turn to him for help and strength, so we will bow to his will in our lives. It takes faith and trust in the Lord to turn our very selves over to him for improvement. We often resist this step, working instead on our own personal to-do list, but tremendous growth starts with humble trust.

3. **Recognize that God can change us.** "And my grace is sufficient for all men that humble themselves before me; for if they humble themselves before me, and have faith in me, then will I make weak things become strong unto them." As we evaluate our weaknesses, we must recognize that God not only can and will, but also *wants* to help us change those weaknesses into strengths.

4. **Come to understand our divine nature.** As we work through converting our weaknesses to strengths, we must come to understand our own ability to change and see ourselves as the daughter of God that we were meant to be.

5. **Ask God for help.** Once we understand our divine relationship with God, we can ask him to "make weak things become strong" and begin progressing toward strength.

6. **Accept strengthening experiences.** The Lord has said that he will make us strong, and often he does this through the strengthening experiences and opportunities that come into our lives such as trials, difficulties, or callings.

7. **Come to see yourself as God sees you.** We come full circle, our weakness transformed into strength, and at that point we realize that our strength is part of who we are. We realize that is how God sees us.

Now let's take this Prophet Formula—this formula for turning weaknesses into strengths—and see how it works through some examples.

Enoch

The first example I'd like to review is the prophet Enoch. I love the prophet Enoch. What's not to love in a shy, unpopular young man who ends up moving mountains with his word and having his city translated? This is a classic story of weakness turning to strength!

We begin in Moses 6:31:

> And when Enoch had heard these words, he bowed himself to the earth, before the Lord, and spake before the Lord, saying: Why is it that I have found favor in thy sight, and am but a lad, and all the people hate me; for I am slow of speech; wherefore am I thy servant?

Enoch recognized his shortcomings. He felt like his weaknesses included the fact he was a poor speaker, he was young and inexperienced, and he was not a popular person. He was well aware of these "weaknesses," and they seemed to him to be serious impediments to becoming a prophet, which was what the Lord was asking him to do.

He asked the Lord, "Wherefore am I thy servant?" Essentially asking "Why me?" He was humble before the Lord. He recognized that he was a weak vessel and was very meek. The story continues,

> And the Lord said unto Enoch: Go forth and do as I have commanded thee, and no man shall pierce thee. Open thy mouth, and it shall be filled, and I will give thee utterance, for all flesh is in my hands, and I will do as seemeth me good.
>
> Say unto this people: Choose ye this day, to serve the Lord God who made you.
>
> Behold my Spirit is upon you, wherefore all thy words will I justify; and the mountains shall flee before you, and the rivers

shall turn from their course; and thou shalt abide in me, and I in you; therefore walk with me.

> And the Lord spake unto Enoch, and said unto him: Anoint thine eyes with clay, and wash them, and thou shalt see. And he did so. (Moses 6:32–35)

Enoch trusted in the Lord and went ahead and did what he was told to do. He recognized that the Lord was all-powerful and could change his weaknesses into strengths. He had complete faith and confidence—not in himself but in his God.

Then Enoch's life was transformed. He became a great seer and prophet.

> Behold, our father Adam taught these things, and many have believed and become the sons of God, and many have believed not, and have perished in their sins, and are looking forth with fear, in torment, for the fiery indignation of the wrath of God to be poured out upon them. (Moses 7:1)

In seeing his own divine nature, he recognized that he could do the things that the Lord had told him he was capable of doing. Enoch faithfully accepted his calling:

> And it came to pass that Enoch went forth in the land, among the people, standing upon the hills and the high places, and cried with a loud voice, testifying against their works; and all men were offended because of him. . . .
>
> And it came to pass when they heard him, no man laid hands on him; for fear came on all them that heard him; for he walked with God. (Moses 6:37, 39)

Using God's help, he was able to do all the things required of him.

Enoch then had tremendous strengthening experiences:

> And so great was the faith of Enoch that he led the people of God, and their enemies came to battle against them; and he spake the word of the Lord, and the earth trembled, and the mountains fled, even according to his command; and the rivers of water

were turned out of their course; and the roar of the lions was heard out of the wilderness; and all nations feared greatly, so powerful was the word of Enoch, and so great was the power of the language which God had given him. (Moses 7:13)

He grew into a mighty prophet of the Lord, able to move mountains and control rivers, so great was his faith in his Heavenly Father.

Finally, Enoch, now fully a strong man of God, was caught up to heaven:

And it came to pass that the Lord showed unto Enoch all the inhabitants of the earth; and he beheld, and lo, Zion, in process of time, was taken up into heaven. And the Lord said unto Enoch: Behold mine abode forever. (Moses 7:21)

Enoch came to see himself as God saw him, as a prophet who would lead his people in such profound righteousness that they were returned to the presence of the Lord.

Enoch changed from a weak and inexperienced young man into a mighty prophet of God whose word was no longer slow, but filled with great power. He was able to make this transformation with the help of the Lord.

Moses

Another prophet who turned his own weakness to strength with the help of the Lord was Moses, who went through this very same process.

In Exodus 3:11, Moses asked the Lord: "Who am I, that I should go unto Pharaoh, and that I should bring forth the children of Israel out of Egypt?" (There's that "why me?" question again.) Later, in Exodus 4:10, he said: "O my Lord, I am not eloquent, neither heretofore, nor since thou hast spoken unto thy servant: but I am slow of speech, and of a slow tongue." Moses recognized and acknowledged to the Lord his shortcomings.

These sound very familiar to us by now: he can't speak well, the people will not accept him either because they don't know who he is or because they won't recognize his authority. He is concerned about these hindrances.

Here again, these perceived weaknesses seem to Moses to be a major impediment for what he is asked to do, which is to become a prophet. A prophet needs to speak well and to lead the people in a way that they will follow.

It has always been interesting to me that Moses was troubled by these "weaknesses" because we know that he was raised in a royal household. It has always kind of surprised me that he had these feelings. I don't know exactly what the weakness was that he was referring to when he told the Lord he was "slow of speech." Maybe he was relatively shy, maybe he had a speech impediment, or maybe he wasn't used to being in front of crowds. Of course, I think anyone who faces the immensity of a calling as a prophet of God might feel that they were slow of speech.

It is interesting to note that the very weaknesses both of these prophets claim are the exact opposite of the strengths needed to do the job they are called to do. God molds them into prophets through this process of changing weaknesses into strengths.

In Moses 1:10, the story continues:

> And it came to pass that it was for the space of many hours before Moses did again receive his natural strength like unto man; and he said unto himself: Now, for this cause I know that man is nothing, which thing I never had supposed.

Moses was brought down into the depths of humility when he considered the enormity of the call being extended to him. He, in comparison, saw himself as very weak. Yet he was given a true understanding of the nature of Heavenly Father's children and realized how "insignificant" his life was in the universe. He also learned that man is not to be feared. I wonder if his fear of Pharaoh disappeared at this moment. Once Moses could see the immensity of God's creations, perhaps Pharaoh just didn't seem that scary anymore.

But now mine own eyes have beheld God; but not my natural, but my spiritual eyes, for my natural eyes could not have beheld; for I should have withered and died in his presence; but his glory was upon me; and I beheld his face, for I was transfigured before him. (Moses 1:11)

Moses recognized that the Lord was all-powerful, and that he could take care of Moses' weaknesses, so that he could accomplish the things that he needed to do in Moses' life.

Then Satan showed up, as he tends to do:

And it came to pass that Moses looked upon Satan and said: Who art thou? For behold, I am a son of God, in the similitude of his Only Begotten; and where is thy glory, that I should worship thee? (Moses 1:13)

When Moses is approached by Satan, he says those great words—"I am a son of God"—and challenges Satan. Moses saw Satan for what he was—an inferior being—and recognized his own divine nature—that he was a son of Deity, a son of God. And this, as we read in the verses that follow, which I find instructive and also personally hilarious, really upsets Satan. Satan has a real hissy fit, stomping all over:

And now Satan began to tremble, and the earth shook; and Moses received strength, and called upon God, saying: In the name of the Only Begotten, depart hence, Satan.

And it came to pass that Satan cried with a loud voice, with weeping, and wailing, and gnashing of teeth; and he departed hence, even from the presence of Moses, that he beheld him not. (Moses 1:21–22)

I believe Satan is always upset when any of us realize our divine nature because it is contrary to everything he would like us to believe about ourselves. He is so upset because Moses truly understands his eternal worth and the power that comes from that understanding.

This is one of my favorite parts in all of the scriptures. Here

Moses has understood "how insignificant" he is in the eternal and universal scheme of things, and yet in the very next verses he also comes to the great understanding of the eternal significance of who he is—a son of God. For the first time, he grasps this concept and recognizes his divine nature. This realization gives him tremendous power and self-confidence.

> And calling upon the name of God, he beheld his glory again, for it was upon him; and he heard a voice, saying: Blessed art thou, Moses, for I, the Almighty, have chosen thee, and thou shalt be made stronger than many waters; for they shall obey thy command as if thou wert God.
>
> And lo, I am with thee, even unto the end of thy days; for thou shalt deliver my people from bondage, even Israel my chosen. (Moses 1:25–26)

Moses learned his lessons well, and this experience is the beginning of Moses' journey from weakness into becoming a strong prophet.

We know that Moses accepted the call and sought the Lord's help in doing what the Lord needed him to do, which was to confront Pharaoh and free the Israelites from bondage. This, too, makes me chuckle. How would it be to face Pharaoh and say, "I've just had a conversation with God." Uh, okay. Do you realize how powerful that is? Moses had direct communion with the Lord and was able to stand there and say that to Pharaoh.

Moses had many, many strengthening experiences. The book of Exodus is filled with them. He was strong enough to confront Pharaoh and call down all the plagues. He organized and led a massive group of people away from bondage. He parted the Red Sea—what a tremendously strengthening experience that must have been! (See Exodus 3–20.)

Moses came to see himself as God saw him: a prophet of God, a leader, and a liberator of his people. He also continued to be taught humility and his relationship with the Lord. Moses was transformed from a weak vessel into a great and mighty prophet of the Lord because he turned his apparent weaknesses into tremendous strengths in the service of his Heavenly Father.

Other Prophets

There are many more examples throughout the scriptures. Others saw Peter as a fisherman; Christ saw him as an apostle and future leader of the Church. Weakness became strength.

Peter often gets a bad rap as a prophet. The experience of his denial of Christ seems to often overshadow his life of dedication and service. We need to keep in mind that sometimes the experiences we are given are going to be experiences in which we fail. This was so for Peter. It was a powerful teaching experience for Peter when he failed to do what was right. He was brought down to great humility in the process, and I think that experience helped him realize how far he still needed to go.

We shouldn't lose sight of the fact that, when Christ is walking on the water, Peter is the only one to actually step out of the boat and begin to walk across the water toward him. Such tremendous faith and trust in the Lord! So, Peter had wonderful strengths in him, they just needed to be refined and developed by the Lord.

Looking at Alma the Younger, some saw him as a weak and destructive teenager. The Lord saw potential for strength. Others perceived Joseph Smith as a poor, uneducated teenager. In fact, Joseph commented on this perception:

> It caused me serious reflection then, and often has since, how very strange it was that an obscure boy, of a little over fourteen years of age, and one, too, who was doomed to the necessity of obtaining a scanty maintenance by his daily labor, should be thought a character of sufficient importance to attract the attention of the great ones of the most popular sects of the day, and in a manner to create in them a spirit of the most bitter persecution and reviling. But strange or not, so it was, and it was often the cause of great sorrow to myself. (Joseph Smith–History 1:23)

And yet, Joseph went on to become the greatest man who ever lived, second only to Jesus Christ. A great man of strength!

Each of these prophets' lives is a lesson and example to us of how we can apply the Prophet Formula to our own lives and change our own weakness into strength. It is a tremendous blessing to us that these stories have been recorded in scripture, so we can see that these prophets didn't start out as mighty, powerful men capable of great miracles, but that they started out as humble people just like us.

We could apply this process to virtually every prophet in recorded scripture and see the transformation that took place. Over and over again this process is repeated throughout the scriptures to teach us that we can and should rise above our weaknesses, turn to the Lord for his help, and come to see ourselves as God sees us.

Personal Application of the Prophet Formula

So let's apply the Prophet Formula to our own lives and see how we can change and improve our own weaknesses and turn them into strengths.

1. Recognize your weakness. Each of us can come up with a long list of what we feel are our weaknesses that we need to work on and improve. But remember, what you perceive as a weakness may only be a difference. This principle was taught to me by a friend who had many children; one son was particularly difficult to raise. She said she came to the understanding that things that she thought he was doing wrong were really only a different way of doing things. His actions didn't violate any commandment, they were just different from the way she thought things should be done.

I was chatting with a small group of women once and one woman asked how we prepared our kids' lunches for school. The variety was incredible! One made them the night before. One gave her kids money to buy lunch. I had my children make their own.

Another lined up her kids and they all did it together. Each one was different and none of them were wrong!

We need to look at this in our own lives. Sometimes we think that what we are doing is a weakness when we compare it to how somebody else does it. Yet it may just be our own unique and different way of doing things. Comparison to others is not the best way to identify our weaknesses. We must compare only to ourselves and ask ourselves, "Is this a weakness in my life? Does it hold me back? Is this behavior or action a detriment to me?"

Another way to identify your weakness is to ask yourself what is hampering your progress. What is it in your behavior or lack of understanding or nature that is keeping you from moving forward in becoming a strong Latter-day Saint? What feels like an impediment? What feels like something you might need to overcome, because if you did, you could progress toward becoming who you need to be? Ask the Lord to help you in this self-reflection.

Next, look at what you're putting off dealing with. This is often a painful examination. But we all know what it is—it's the change we list every New Year's Day as our goal: "This year, I'm going to develop patience"; or, "This year I'm going to study my scriptures more"; or, "This year I'll be more charitable." We roll the same goal over every year to the next year and promise to deal with it later. These things are often deeply ingrained personality traits. So take the time to write them down and face them.

You can also look to your patriarchal blessing and see what is unfulfilled. There are certain events, certain attributes that are foretold in our patriarchal blessing. As you read through those promises, see which ones have not come to pass yet. Think about who you could become or what you need to be doing in order for that patriarchal blessing to be fulfilled. Remember, that special blessing is how God sees us, and so long as we work on those things that will lead us toward the fulfillment of those blessings, we can become who we are meant to be.

In addition, our patriarchal blessing will identify warnings for us of things that we need to beware of. This too can be a way to identify a weak area in our spiritual development so we can tackle it head-on and begin to transform it into a strength.

Also, ask Heavenly Father what one thing you should work on—but be prepared for the answer! Heavenly Father knows us the very best, and he also knows what we need to work on and develop—and in what order—to prepare us to complete our mission on the earth. Ask him! We may not always want to hear his answer, but he will always tell us what one thing he would like us to work on in developing a weakness into a strength.

Finally, avoid a laundry list. Sometimes when we undertake an effort to change, we create a long list of things we need to work on and improve. That list can be very counterproductive because we look at it and think, "Ugh, I have so much to do and so much to change, I don't know where to begin." We get bogged down before we even begin. So rather than stare at a daunting list, select just one or two that are a high priority for you and start there.

2. Become humble before God. "And inasmuch as they were humble they might be made strong, and blessed from on high, and receive knowledge from time to time" (D&C 1:28).

The key ingredient to change is to be humble before God, to be aware of our need to change and of our weakness before him. We can't fool him; he knows all. He knows quite clearly what our imperfections are. We can fool other people into thinking that we are the epitome of patience or that we are charitable, but the Lord knows our heart and sees our real weaknesses clearly.

If you're not prepared to hear a painful or difficult answer, then it may be that you're not yet humble enough. Sometimes we hesitate to pray to our Heavenly Father about our weaknesses because we're hanging on to them, and we don't want to change because we're comfortable where we are. We're not yet ready to hear what he has to say to us about changing because we're afraid it will be too hard. This is a key indicator that we have not yet humbled ourselves enough to cause a change in our life and that perhaps we need to focus on our humility first.

One of the defining characteristics of all the prophets is their humility toward God. They are willing to submit, as the scriptures say, as a child submits to his father (see Mosiah 3:19). They receive counsel from the Lord and are willing to do whatever he says. So, too, in our lives, we need to be completely humble and willing to submit to the Lord's will. We need to be humble enough to the point where we can be receptive to the answers to our prayers—even difficult answers.

3. Recognize that God can change us. We need to understand that Heavenly Father wants to help us, and that we are worth his time and attention. I think of helping our own children with their homework. If a child comes to us and says, "I need help with my math homework," do we mock them and say, "Oh, man, you are so dumb!" or "Can't you figure this out?" or "I already helped you with this!" Never would any of us say anything like that to our own children, and yet sometimes we're afraid of our Heavenly Father's reaction to our own weaknesses.

Sometimes we don't feel that we are worthy of his help. One of the defining characteristics of our Heavenly Father is that he dearly loves his children. We know that he is all-powerful. We know that he controls the universe. And yet sometimes we doubt his willingness or his ability to bring about change in our own lives. We must rely on the fact that he is perfectly able to completely change us. He has helped millions of our brothers and sisters change their lives. He will help us if we will only let him.

Elder Neal A. Maxwell said, "By playing upon the weaknesses of men, the adversary can easily persuade many that these weaknesses are so congenital that they cannot (indeed, need not) be overcome."[5] This is especially true in our day. We constantly read in the media that many of the weaknesses and behavioral choices that people are making are practically genetic. I remember discussing this once with a science teacher. I was concerned about the curriculum and what was going to be taught in the classroom. He went on and on, saying, "Don't you know that this is genetic? Don't you know that this controls the way that people behave? They have no control over their own behavior."

I thought, *No, the case has not been made that these choices are genetic*. Satan would love for us to believe that we can't change ourselves. He would love for us to believe that our weaknesses are so embedded in our character that they are impossible to change. This is a falsehood from the adversary. We must recognize and believe to the core of our being that our Heavenly Father can change our weaknesses.

4. Come to understand our divine nature. Each of us needs to come to understand who we really are and what our divine nature really is. It is my humble opinion that each of us has what I would call "God DNA." In our spirits, there is the potential for all the capabilities and faculties of our Heavenly Father and our Heavenly Mother.

We need to understand and recognize that we are queens in the kingdom of God. That is the true destiny of our mortal existence. As we come to believe at a deep level in our divine nature and in our divine worth, our perception of our weaknesses changes completely.

When we do not have this understanding, we look at our weaknesses from the bottom up. From that perspective, it seems rather daunting, like looking at a mountain from its base. We are at a low, weak level, and we look up at the change needed and think, "Oh, that's so hard. That's so beyond where I am." Or we think something like, "Making this change is going to be so difficult, I don't know if I can do it."

As we come to embrace our divine nature, however, our perspective completely changes and we can look at our weaknesses from the top down. If I perceive myself as a queen in the kingdom of heaven and as a daughter of God, then I look at my weaknesses and think, "Oh, these silly weaknesses. . . . I want to improve them and make them strong, so I can bring my behavior and my skills and abilities up to the level of who I really am—a daughter of God."

Our weaknesses look much less insurmountable this way. In fact, it just looks more like a course correction, or simply bringing all our skills, behaviors, and choices into line with who we really are. It seems like a much easier process when we approach it from the top looking down.

Christ never had a problem with self-esteem. Why? He knew he was the Son of God. He knew from the time he was a child that he was very literally the Only Begotten of the Father. This truth stayed with him his whole life in such a powerful way that he never had doubts about it, even when he was tempted by Satan. He never had concerns when he was approached by members of the community, including powerful politicians and other leaders. He knew who he was. As a result, he had tremendous self-esteem. He understood his divine nature. Understanding our divine nature is our key to changing our weakness into strength.

5. Ask God for help. In Doctrine and Covenants 82:10 we read, "I, the Lord, am bound when ye do what I say; but when ye do not what I say, ye have no promise." Understanding this scripture is a key element in having our Heavenly Father assist us in this process. How do we bind the Lord? Read the verse again. He is bound *when we do what he says.*

This first step in asking for Heavenly Father's help is key. Let's say, for example, you have a problem with parenting. Perhaps you are feeling this problem is hampering the progress of you and your family. Now, in following this verse, we must do what the Lord says. What has he said to do? Here is a short list, by no means comprehensive. (I call this the "family five.") First of all, hold family prayer, recommended twice a day. Second, hold regular family home evenings with our families. Third, take our families to church with us faithfully. Fourth, have daily scripture study in our home. Fifth, have family recreational activities where the family spends time having fun together.

Now, if we want to improve our parenting, we do what the Lord says. We do these five things to the best of our abilities, as best as we know how. Then what? Then we can go to our Heavenly Father and tell him, "We're struggling with parenting, with our children. I've done all these things that thou hast told me to do with my family. I need thy help." Define what the problem is, and then ask for his help.

At this point, Heavenly Father is bound to help us, and he will.

The second half of that verse is also true. When we don't do what he says, we don't have a promise. I wonder how many bishops would say they have met with parents who have come to them and say they are having trouble with their family. Perhaps one of the first questions a bishop might ask is, "Are you having family prayer?"

"Well, no, we're too busy. We don't really have time to do that."

"Are you having family home evenings?"

"Well, no, the teenagers don't want to come and my husband travels a lot."

Those words in the Doctrine and Covenants mean something when they say, "when ye do not what I say, ye have no promise." If we first do what the Lord says, then we will be blessed.

This promise applies to every commandment. If we want to be blessed with great health and strength, we must first do what the Lord says and keep the Word of Wisdom and the spirit of the Word of Wisdom. Then he is bound to bless us and help us when we ask.

If we would like to understand the scriptures better, we must first study them and feast upon the words of Christ, as he has told us. Only then can we bind the Lord and ask for his help.

We can see where this pattern is leading and what the results are—if we identify a weakness and one or two (or several) commandments that apply to that weakness, and then if we apply all our efforts to keeping those commandments, what will happen? The truth is that if we do what the Lord says, most of our weaknesses and concerns will largely resolve themselves.

Let me repeat that. As we do what the Lord says and keep his commandments, most of our weaknesses and concerns will resolve themselves. Now some will not, and we'll still struggle with them. But because of our honest obedience and effort, the Lord is bound and we can ask for his help. We can say we are doing the best we know how in keeping the commandments surrounding our weakness, but that we still need help. He then comes immediately to our aid to bless us.

In Alma 26:10–12 it reads:

> And it came to pass that when Ammon had said these words, his brother Aaron rebuked him, saying: Ammon, I fear that thy joy doth carry thee away unto boasting.
>
> But Ammon said unto him: I do not boast in my own strength, nor in my own wisdom; but behold, my joy is full, yea, my heart is brim with joy, and I will rejoice in my God.
>
> Yea, I know that I am nothing; as to my strength I am weak; therefore I will not boast of myself, but I will boast of my God, for in his strength I can do all things; yea, behold, many mighty miracles we have wrought in this land, for which we will praise his name forever.

Ammon is accused by his brother of boasting of the Lord. But Ammon tells him that he was called in the strength of the Lord and can do all things. With our Heavenly Father's help, we, too, can do all things.

6. Accept strengthening experiences. An important part of turning our weaknesses into strengths is having strengthening experiences where our weak attributes are challenged and tested and improved upon and refined until they become strengths in our lives. In Doctrine and Covenants 50:16, it says, "I will be merciful unto you; he that is weak among you hereafter shall be made strong." I want to emphasize those words: "hereafter shall be made strong."

We as daughters and saints of God are being made strong through opportunities that come our way to stretch us and make us grow. If we reject those experiences as being too difficult or undesirable, then that strengthening will not occur.

We need to accept those experiences, as difficult and painful as they might be, and say, "Isn't this wonderful? I'm getting an opportunity to work on something that was weak and make it strong."

Think of what builds a strong tree. Some of the strongest trees grow in areas where they are buffeted by the wind and where they have to resist the wind's force and grow into strength. Think of tempered steel and the tremendous heat that is required to make such a strong metal. It is that wind, heat, and fire that are the strengthening experiences that we need to go through.

Sometimes those experiences are thrust upon us. My dear friend Sue was diagnosed with breast cancer. It was certainly something that was thrust upon her, and yet she chose to go through that experience and look at it as an opportunity to develop strength in her life. She developed great patience with herself and her family. Her faith was made stronger as she went through the ordeal. It also gave her a tremendous insight into the eternal perspective. She said, "You know, when you get that diagnosis, all your worldly cares about your weight, possessions, or money issues just fall away and you get down to the strength of your relationship with your Heavenly Father. That is what truly matters." Even when some difficult experiences come to us involuntarily, we can still choose to grow from them.

My husband once lost his job at a time when the economy was slowing down, and his area of work was in a recession. We knew that this situation would probably be lengthy, and early on I said, "We can choose to be bitter and upset and worry through this entire experience, or we can look at this as an opportunity to grow." We identified several things that we wanted to develop and learn during this time so that we could use it as a strengthening experience for us and our family.

One of the greatest results we enjoyed was that after spending a long time home with the family, my husband grew in his love for his sons and in his love for our family, and we all became so much closer. The experience blessed our family in many ways, including strengthening our belief in and love for the prophet. We had been counseled to have a year's supply, and thankfully, our family had one in place when this happened.

There were other unexpected blessings as well. Because my

husband enjoyed being home so much when he was looking for a job, he tried to find one where he could still work from home. He was successful in his search, and ever since then my husband has worked from home for various companies. It has been a tremendous blessing to our family.

When we look back at the experience of my husband's unemployment, we think, "That could have been very debilitating, but instead it was such a tremendous growing experience, and we grew in so many ways that it was, in fact, a great blessing in our life." As you look at your own experiences, learn to ask, "What can I gain from this? What can I learn from this? How can I grow from this? What weakness can this help me develop into a strength?"

Sometimes it is helpful to ask ourselves what activities we could voluntarily add to our lives that might help us overcome a weakness. Look at the weaknesses that you have identified that you want to change, and think of experiences that would transform, test, and challenge them in your life. Perhaps you feel shy around large groups of people—maybe you could volunteer to help out in the school classroom. Perhaps you are working on developing patience—maybe you could work with developmentally disabled young adults. Perhaps you wish you were more nurturing—maybe you could help with the young babies during sacrament meeting. There are many experiences you could add to your life that could help you develop a weakness into a strength.

I have to wonder if sometime early in my life I asked the Lord to put some growth opportunities into my life to help teach me patience. He willingly complied by sending me four sons. Trust me, I have *really* learned patience! With any weakness we can identify, there are certain experiences that will help develop that attribute into a strength.

In asking our Heavenly Father to send strengthening experiences into our lives, we need to be careful because he will answer that prayer. We need to be bold in accepting the opportunities he sends to us and grow from them. If we ask him for help, but then run terrified in the other direction and don't embrace those opportunities, we will definitely lose the benefits that could have been ours.

7. Come to see yourself as God sees you. As we go through these experiences, we need come to see ourselves as God sees us. In other words, we need to learn to perceive our desired strengths as already a part of us. One of the ways we can do this, of course, is to read our patriarchal blessing on a regular basis. The truth is our Father in Heaven's eternal perspective allows him to see in us those strengths that we want to develop. They may have been strengths that we had in the premortal life that are part of our nature. We need to see ourselves as already possessing great strength.

One of the things that will help us is if we cease to compare ourselves to others. Often we compare our weakness to another person's strength and end up feeling unhappy with our progress. What we may not see is our budding strength and incredible personal growth. Father knows us for who we are and who we can become. As we cease to compare ourselves to others, we will be able to see our true selves revealed.

We can move from weakness to strength. If we suffer from uncertainty or worry or fear, we can develop the strength of faith. If we have lives that are chaotic, or if we procrastinate, we can develop organizational skills. If we are unstudied, we can become great lovers of scripture. If we are selfish, greedy, or demanding, we can develop the strength of charity. If we are impatient and irritable, we can develop patience.

So, go back to the list of weaknesses that you want to overcome. Rewrite them by putting your name in and filling in the strength you are working toward. For example, perhaps you worry that you suffer from the weakness of self-centeredness. As you commit to change that, write "Mary is kind in her feelings towards others." Even the simple act of reading those affirmations can help us move toward becoming Women of Strength.

Ultimately, we are Women of Strength when we keep ourselves on the path of self-improvement, guided by deep faith. As we are true to our core spirit, our abilities and divine attributes will surface and grow. We will continue to chip away at the weaknesses that we find in ourselves, and what will be left is a Woman of Strength, well-equipped to serve in the kingdom and live a life of great joy.

CHAPTER 7

Women of Eternity,
Not Mortality

It was Thanksgiving Day and I was reviewing the sales ads just out of idle curiosity. Frankly, I couldn't think of a single thing I needed. (Going to Africa has that effect on you.) But then I saw it. A red leather jacket. A really *cute* red leather jacket. At a really, really great price. I wanted it. But I talked myself out of it.

Later that evening, I was watching TV and an ad came on for the same store. And there it was again! That great red leather jacket. And it was even cuter on a real person! Did I mention that I *love* red? I have a red car, tons of red clothes, red everything. I have red throughout my house, including the bright red office chair I sit in to write! When I campaigned for public office, my colors were red and white. So I was *majorly* attracted to that jacket.

Now to be honest, I already had a red leather jacket. I know, I know—but this new one was so *cute!* It zipped up, and the one I had buttoned. Clearly, I *needed* another red jacket. I knew I would wear it all the time. I travel a lot and leather is great for traveling. And seriously, the price was really, really great.

The whole family got a good laugh out of the stores running sales at ridiculously early hours. (Come on—who goes shopping at 4 AM? Isn't that a little over the top?) So the next morning I got up to go buy that red leather jacket. I waited until a decent hour—6 AM. I'm not crazy, after all.

I went into the store and made a beeline for the jacket section. There it was! And it fit beautifully. I happily hung the red jacket on my arm and headed for the check-out counter. After all, I really didn't need anything else.

But then I saw the shiny shirts. They, too, were on sale at a really, really great price. I had wanted a shiny shirt because they look great when I speak on stage. So I picked out three and happily hung them on my arm.

I almost made it to the check-out counter when I saw the skirts. Couldn't pass them up. The prices were incredible! And my Christmas sweaters could stand a new addition as well.

On and on it went. After a while, my arm was tired from holding everything and I hung up all my fabulous, couldn't-live-without-them items on an empty rack by the dressing room. Off I went with arms free to gather more! (And yes, some very organized employee put everything away so I had to go hunt it all down again. I guess I had strayed too far from keeping an eye on my selections.)

Three hours later I staggered to the counter with a pile of items that were all at really, really great prices! The cashier chuckled as I justified everything she rang up. The final total was just ridiculous. Out I went with four huge bags slung over my arms. I threw them in the back of the red Mother Ship.

I got in the van and paused. Then I burst out laughing. For a woman who didn't need a thing, I had sure found a lot of "needed" items!

Now, lest you think I'm a total glutton, I did return many items when I regained my sanity. But I kept the red jacket. I'm not stupid. I wear it all the time!

So let us recap, shall we? Take a big sale, add some great prices, sprinkle in a bit of shopping frenzy, and what do you get? A Woman of Mortality.

It's a little disconcerting to think of that title: A Woman of Mortality.

But let's face it. There is a constant pull every moment of every day to deal with the concerns of mortality.

This earthly life is very demanding. We have to make sure we have a safe place to live. We need to feed ourselves and our families. We have to have clothes. We need to have a way to provide for these necessities. Plus we need to take care of our health, both physical and mental. We need to be aware of and involved in social interactions. We need to clean everything. And sometimes we need to take a break from it all. That's a full life's work!

Mortality is also very subtle. If we have to have a place to live, can't it be as big as we can afford? Or barely afford? And we need relaxation. Just think of how much *more* relaxation and family interaction we can have with a big-screen TV and home theater system. It'll only take 324 payments of $49.95. So cheap!

Mortality takes work. There is no escaping that fact.

Physical Bodies

This leads me to a very important part of mortality: our bodies. This was the big reward for choosing to come here. And it's great. But this body of mine takes a lot of work and sometimes has a mind of its own!

Elder Russell M. Nelson speaks of the human body as only a doctor can:

> Think of the most magnificent sight you have ever seen. . . .
> . . . These magnificent sights are wondrous beyond measure. They are all "great deeds" of our divine Creator.
> Now, ponder the magnificence of what you see when you look in the mirror. Ignore the freckles, the unruly hair, or the blemishes, and look beyond to see the real you—a child of God—created by him, in his image. If we lift the lid on the treasure chest of the marvelous attributes of our bodies, we can discover, at least in part, the magnificence of man.[1]

Having a mortal body is a distinct challenge. We have to feed it. We have to dress it. We have to exercise it. And we have to deal with all the appetites and passions that are triggered by having an earthly body. Not easy tasks. In fact, our bodies are really high maintenance, and managing them is something most of us struggle with.

In my legal career, I handle estates after people die. So I deal with death often, and it is always sad when that death comes earlier than it should have. I once sat with a family while the father, a chain-smoker, was told he had two days to live. He was only 63. And his wife sat strapped securely in a wheelchair at the age of 62 because her lifelong smoking habit had triggered a stroke. I told the children—all smokers—that this habit had cost their family probably twenty years of life and love with their parents. I begged them all to stop so that *their* children would not have to pay the same price.

In 2003, the Cedar Wildfires in California destroyed fifty-four homes in my city. Half a dozen fire victims were heavy smokers. Every single one of them was dead within one year. In 2007, the Witchcreek Wildfires destroyed ninety homes. Within two weeks, a fire victim who had been a heavy smoker was dead due to a massive stroke. I learned that compromised bodies do not survive stress well.

Other clients suffer from the effects of obesity. One client has had multiple strokes and has major diabetes. Another has diabetes and congestive heart failure. Both could die as many as twenty years earlier than normal. Their bodies have deteriorated significantly as a result of choosing not to control their eating or exercise.

Our bodies take effort. Women of Eternity realize that there is an integral connection between our bodies and our spirits. We must learn to care for our bodies and control our passions so that we are fit for service. We have been given a precious gift from our Heavenly Father. Neglecting that gift is to our peril.

But some of us are so swept up in the world that we place

inordinate importance on our appearance. "How do I look?" is more important than "How do I behave?"

My son, Connor, blogged about this idea when he posted a picture of an African boy seeing himself in a mirror for the first time:

> What would it be like to have never seen yourself? How would life be different without a reflection? Would we see ourselves differently? How would we dress? Would we spend our time and money on cosmetics and such superficiality?
>
> It's stunning to realize that some people have never seen themselves before. How would you, having lived in a remote African village without any mirror or shiny surface with which to see your own face?
>
> A mirror changes things. Like the (anonymous) quote goes, "When man found the mirror, he began to lose his soul."[2]

Later, Connor elaborated on this idea,

> Such a simple statement conveys a very profound principle. Our decadent society has become wholly self-indulgent and all too focused on the image of self.
>
> This trend is not without its associated consequences.

Connor then quotes Victor B. Cline, who stated,

> I am convinced by a vast amount of research that the images, fantasies, and models which we are repeatedly exposed to in advertisements, entertainment, novels, motion pictures, and other works of art can and do . . . affect the self-image and, later, the behavior of nearly all young people and adults too.[3]

Connor then quotes Sister Susan W. Tanner:

> [She] commented on what she sees as a troubling practice of "making over" what is deemed socially unacceptable.
>
> "I am troubled by the practice of extreme makeovers. Happiness comes from accepting the bodies we have been given as divine gifts and enhancing our natural attributes, not from remaking our bodies after the image of the world. The Lord wants us to be made over—but in His image, not in the image of

the world, by receiving His image in our countenances (see Alma 5:14, 19)."⁴

Connor concludes by saying,

> Are we fostering such a materialistic, superficial view of our bodies and images by patronizing and supporting related TV shows, magazines, and department stores that tout beauty as something that can be bought?
>
> What garbage.⁵

To be honest, this is spoken by a man. He has no idea how hard it is to be a woman! Just the hair and make-up and nails and clothes and shoes alone take enormous effort, right?

We must strike a balance in having a fit and healthy body without obsessing about our weight. We must strike a balance in giving appropriate attention to keeping ourselves attractive without falling into the trap of vanity and pride. It is good to ponder the management of our bodies, and this takes some honest reflection.

Living in the world is tricky business, and the business of living requires that we pay attention to the world in which we live. We're encouraged to be successful and work hard. The fruits of that effort usually show up in tangible ways, and it's hard to say categorically that all of it is bad or wrong.

I think we can all acknowledge that, at some level, worldliness is a bad thing. Elder Neal A. Maxwell discussed this in his talk, "The Tugs and Pulls of the World":

> For true believers, the tugs and pulls of the world—including its pleasures, power, praise, money, and preeminence—have always been there. Now, however, many once-helpful support systems are bent or broken. Furthermore, the harmful things of the world are marketed by pervasive technology and hyped by a media barrage, potentially reaching almost every home and hamlet. All this when many are already tuned out of spiritual things, saying, "I am rich, . . . increased with goods, and have need of nothing" (Rev. 3:17) . . .

. . . God's plan is not the plan of pleasure; it is the "plan of happiness."

The tugs and pulls of the world are powerful. Worldly lifestyles are cleverly reinforced by the rationalization, "Everybody is doing it," thus fanning or feigning a majority. . . .

Peter counseled, "Of whom a man is overcome, of the same is he brought in bondage" (2 Pet. 2:19). Brothers and sisters, there are so many personalized prisons![6]

Dealing with the tugs and pulls of the world can be difficult. It is hard to know, sometimes, how far is too far.

My children and I were having this discussion one day. We were talking about what would be an appropriately-sized home to own. I related to them a case we had had before the city council. A person had applied for a permit to develop his property. The house was to be more than 10,000 square feet and situated on a very prominent hill. The separate "gym" building was to be 2,500 square feet. And the separate garage was to be 1,800 square feet. The children were rather shocked when they realized three of our average-sized home would fit into this single home. The conversation took an interesting turn when my son, Brennan, who had lived in Africa all summer, commented that an entire village could live in this gigantic home.

We also discussed President Gordon B. Hinckley's counsel that we buy a "modest" home and pay it off as quickly as possible.[7] All agreed that 10,000 square feet was certainly not modest. We then discussed what size would be considered modest.

Finally, I said to them jokingly, "Okay, boys. You are not permitted to live in a home larger than 4,000 square feet. Everyone promise?" Everyone readily agreed that they would abide by that. I laughed because I knew that with as much time as we had spent serving others in Africa, my boys would be hard-pressed to justify a large home within our family!

But the world works on us constantly. "We have several children and they each need their own room." "We can afford a nicer home." "We need to look successful for our business." "This house isn't as big as the Swenson's." On and on we go, justifying a bigger and bigger home with each step. Then, the rationale gets to be a little silly—"We need a really big area so that the ward can have parties here."

But the world works this way. Step by step. Bit by bit. Until we've crossed that line into firm Woman of Mortality territory.

Perspective

One of the areas where we feel the influence of mortality the greatest is in our perspective. Our attitudes toward what is appropriate or important are majorly affected by the world. After all, we live here! We're on this earth, and the needs of the world are in our face every day.

Just look at the amount of advertising we're exposed to. It is enormous.

> The average American is exposed to about 3000 advertising messages a day, and globally corporations spend over $620 billion each year to make their products seem desirable and to get us to buy them.[8]

> According to the Nielsen Report the average American home had the TV set on for about seven hours a day. The actual viewing was estimated at 4.5 daily hours per adult. To this had to be added radio, which offered 100 words per minute and was listened to an average of two hours a day, mainly in the car. An average daily newspaper offered 150,000 words and it was estimated to take between 18 and 49 minutes of daily reading time. While magazines were browsed over for about 6 to 30 minutes. . . . Media exposure is cumulative . . . All in all, the average adult American uses 6.43 hours a day in media attention. . . . The media, particularly radio and television, have become the audiovisual environment with which we interact endlessly and automatically.[9]

I compare the world of my youth, when TV viewing was infrequent and the Internet was nonexistent, with the world my children live in today. Today, we are constantly being bathed in worldly influences. They are everywhere.

Consider something for a moment with me. What if I were to tell you that I have a wonderful box full of games to play that you could have in your home? It is *amazing* and so real and lifelike. And it's so fun! It will teach your children remarkable things like

- how to waste large amounts of time,
- how to be aggressive and competitive,
- how to kill, maim, and destroy,
- how to eat junk food and put on weight,
- how to be greedy and spend *lots* of money,
- how to be lazy and self-centered,
- how to give up lots of physical activities,
- how to really cut back or eliminate recreational reading,
- how to ignore their parents when they call.

Plus, this magical box of games will keep them so entertained they won't hear the still, small voice when it comes.

Wouldn't that be wonderful?

I ask you, as a Woman of Eternity, why would you *ever* invite this into your home?

And yet, I can guarantee that the vast majority of homes, including LDS homes, have this box enshrined in their midst.

I will make a bold statement here and now. Some will not agree with me, but I believe that every woman who wants her family to be centered in the gospel should throw out the video game systems in her home—and throw them out where they cannot be retrieved.

But it is amazing to me how many women justify having these terrible toys in their homes.

"The kids would get mad if we did that."

"Do you always give in when your children get mad?"

"No. But my husband loves to play games too."

I always ask, "Do you enjoy it when your husband is glued to that thing?"

"No."

Hasn't the world done a magnificent job of convincing so many families that a video game system is necessary? I ask mothers what the positive benefits are of having that box in their home and they are hard-pressed to come up with any. I think often it boils down to, "It keeps the kids occupied so they don't bug me so much." Now *there's* a worthy reason.

I know that the whole premise of this book is to toss the guilt, but as you can tell, I have strong feelings about this topic. So I apologize if I just dumped some unexpected guilt on your head, but this is serious business.

I think the time we waste playing video games is a glaring example of the chains of the world that bind us so absolutely. Add to that the fact that many of us have computers and TVs in every room in the house—including the kids' rooms (a *huge* no-should-do)—and iPods with their tentacles firmly entrenched in the ears of our youth, and you can begin to see how worldly technology has thoroughly infiltrated and infested our lives and our families.

The average American child spends more time watching TV than attending school.

By age 70, the average person will have spent 7 to 10 years of his life watching television.

Just think of all the other things we could be doing to improve ourselves and the country—bike riding, volunteering at a soup kitchen, reading, gardening, playing—instead of sitting frozen in front of TV shows that are often violent, often cruel, and often meaningless.

How troublesome has it become? Increasingly, the television has moved from the family room into the kitchen and into children's bedrooms, often acting as a baby-sitter or substitute friend. Americans now average 2.4 TVs per household, according to the last census. And the effects are pernicious: Studies show that television can contribute to poor grades, obesity, and sleep and behavior problems in children. But that's not all: TV violence is epidemic. Before finishing grade school, the average child will witness about 8,000 murders depicted on TV. Pundits and scientists can debate whether such viewing changes how children act, but let common sense prevail here. Do we really want our children to see this much violence and hatred, especially in the name of entertainment?[10]

And we wonder why our focus is so much on the things of the world? How can it not be?

Not long ago, I went to Africa for three weeks. No cell phones. No TV. No radio. Internet only a few minutes a day. And you know what was really strange? Time. I could not believe how much *time* we had! It took a few days of withdrawals to adjust (I'm a computer junkie), but even with all the hours and hours of work we were doing, we still had all this time.

The other thing that surprised me was my mind. There was space there! I had tons of what I call "brain space." It was amazing. I wasn't worried about the latest political issue. I wasn't thinking over the plotline of the TV show from the night before. I wasn't fretting over the terrible news report of the day. I had all this brain space that was free! That really surprised me. I had no idea how much the very thoughts of my head were driven by the influence of the world.

I had this amazing time to ponder. I could think all on my own. I thought about my family. I thought about the orphans we were caring for. I thought about the plan of salvation. It was remarkable how much deep reflection I was able to do without all that noise in my head.

It is shocking to me how much the world influences our attitudes and perspectives. It is also amazing to me how much I didn't even realize it until I was able to escape from it for a time. That is scary to me. How much of our lives and perceptions have we handed over unwittingly? Way too much.

Possessions

As you might expect, the stark contrast of living in an impoverished nation for a time was very revealing. And yes, while I stood under the freezing cold shower (actually, it was just an elevated pipe emitting a pathetic stream of cold water), I sure did miss my hot shower at home. As I sat in the dirt in a remote bush village, I was extremely grateful for my beautiful house and furniture back home. And while there is no doubt that I was grateful for (and missed!) my rich, tangible blessings at home, I was also struck with how much happiness could be had with so little.

My son Connor wrote:

> This summer I had the opportunity to go on a three-week service trip to Zambia, Africa. What I witnessed was nothing short of a miracle in my mind: a destitute people, lucky to have one meal a day, and owning little more than what you could carry in a backpack. Poor living conditions, meager access to water, and a 94% unemployment rate. And yet, despite their struggles and temporal setbacks, these people showed me what an "attitude of gratitude" is.[11]

How much are we possessed by our possessions? I certainly know I am! I came home from Africa and looked in my closet and was appalled. I have enough clothes for an entire village! I went through my closet and donated a bunch of clothes, but I've noticed that the quantity is creeping up again. How dumb is that?

Nationwide, there are 1.2 cars for every licensed driver. The average U.S. household owns 25 consumer electronic products, including 2.4 TVs.

I'd like you to take a moment to do a little experiment. Pretend that you are a woman in Africa, living in a simple village. Imagine your tiny house, your little kitchen area. Now, stand up and walk through every room of your house and look at what you own. Take the time to look in each closet and every drawer. Startling, isn't it?

I had this experience after coming home from Africa. My sister went to Zambia the same summer and a few days after she came home, she stopped by the store. She walked in and literally had to turn and walk out. She did better than I did. I walked into the store, stood there, and burst into tears. That day I saw the store as one of my African sisters would have seen it, and it was overwhelming. It took months for me to be able to go back to the store without crying my way through the aisles. Even now, those feelings rush back to me.

Now I'm certainly not suggesting that we donate everything we have and move to a third-world country. But we must be aware of the pull of the world with respect to possessions. Our possessions often possess us!

Think of how much time we spend buying things, storing things, cleaning things, rearranging things, and donating things. Things. Things. Everywhere!

Somehow, I don't think the hymn advises, "Because I have been given much, I too must hoard!"

So what is the proper role of possessions in our lives? I think President Gordon B. Hinckley's admonition regarding purchasing a "modest" home that we can afford is a good standard to use.[12] Are our possessions modest and ones we can afford? Or have we gotten out of control?

I would encourage you to take some time to be more aware and to ponder how much the world has influenced you through your possessions. That awareness alone has a way of moderating our behavior.

We can reflect on our definition of "need." There is a hilarious scene in the movie *What About Bob?* where the neurotic Bob begs his psychiatrist for attention: "I *need*, I *need*, I *need!* Gimme, gimme, gimme!" Sometimes, when I find myself shopping, I think of this (Bob's words echoing in my head in the most pathetic, whining voice possible) and I laugh. I also imitate him when my children are in a begging mode. It works wonders.

Often, we blur the lines between needs and wants. Again, awareness is key. A great way to add a course correction in your life is to have some trigger to remind you of the necessary perspective. I have a picture over my desk of the Zambian orphans we served, sitting on the dirt outside their home. Looking at it, I am reminded that possessions are certainly not that important in life. (And also, I am challenged to ask myself, do I really need a *third* red leather jacket? Or would those dollars serve a child in need so much better?)

There is another aspect regarding possessions that I also find troubling. The north part of our city is very wealthy. (There are many people who have garages larger than my home.) The east side of our city is more middle-class and upper middle-class. In 2007, wildfires swept through our city and destroyed ninety homes, about half in the east and about half in the north. More than 60% of the homes destroyed were more than 5,000 square feet. The last time wildfires hit our city (in 2003), they hit the southern part of our city that is a lower income area.

I helped coordinate the fire relief efforts for both fires, and the Witchcreek Wildfires felt vastly different. Even the difference in the reactions of many people between the two fires was interesting. And yet, there was good reason. In the Cedar Wildfires of 2003, more than half of the victims impacted were uninsured and more than half were renters. In the Witchcreek Wildfires of 2007, no homeowners were uninsured and there were only a handful of renters.

After about a month, I was discussing fire relief efforts with the mayor.

"Everyone's okay, aren't they?" he commented.

"Not really," I said.

"Well, they're all rich, aren't they?"

Now I must admit, I had some of those feelings as well. I was distributing checks from the donations that had poured in to the families impacted by the fire. One woman pulled up in a convertible BMW and was wearing huge diamonds on her ears and fingers. And yes, I thought, *Sheesh. You don't need this money.* I shared this experience with my husband and he chastised me, "Merrilee, rich people suffer, too." And I had to admit he was right. These families had lost virtually everything they owned in a devastating disaster. Rich, poor, or in between. It didn't matter. They all suffered.

Our possessions do not and should not define us. More does

not make us better and less does not make us worse. But more or less, our inordinate focus on them can be toxic.

Priorities

Finally, a seriously damaging impact of worldliness is on our priorities. Elder Dallin H. Oaks addressed the issue of priorities in a November 2007 conference address entitled "Good, Better, Best."

> Most of us have more things expected of us than we can pos-sibly do. As breadwinners, as parents, as Church workers and members, we face many choices on what we will do with our time and other resources.
>
> We should begin by recognizing the reality that just because something is *good* is not a sufficient reason for doing it. The number of good things we can do far exceeds the time available to accomplish them. Some things are better than good, and these are the things that should command priority attention in our lives.[13]

Now he could have just as easily entitled his talk, "Evil, Bad, Lousy, Good, Better, Best"! We have so much competing for our time and attention!

Scripture study, shopping at the mall, spending time with kids and family, spending time on entertainment (movies, games, TV, etc.), daily prayer, visiting teaching, temple attendance . . . the list seems endless and every day it seems we are faced with more options, more things to choose from, more ways to spend our time.

Remember, each day we can choose what to do with our time. Each of us has the same amount of time. And each of us needs to determine what our priorities are for us.

The choices are ours. And yes, we need to have balance in our lives. But how often do we neglect the best because we've priori-tized the lousy?

Elder Oaks is clear,

Some uses of individual and family time are better, and others are best. We have to forego some good things in order to choose others that are better or best because they develop faith in the Lord Jesus Christ and strengthen our families.[14]

But here's the wonderful thing about being a Woman of Eternity. We can start at any point! And we can commit to improve at any point! We don't have to beat ourselves up over past mistakes and poor choices, but instead we can toss the guilt and start anew.

I'll share four ways that have helped me to keep my focus on being a Woman of Eternity.

Tie In

The first way to keep our focus on eternal perspectives is to "tie in" each day. Every single day, we must tie ourselves back to our Heavenly Father. I've found the best way to do this is, of course, daily spiritual habits of prayer and scripture.

The following story is another great example of this.

> Gwen, a young woman diagnosed with a serious illness, learned a great deal about diet and nutrition as she diligently followed her doctor's instructions during a year of difficult medical treatment. She studied what she ate with a care that had never been a part of her life until that time. . . .
>
> But as Gwen struggled with her illness, she discovered that the habits of scripture study, regular temple attendance, and daily prayer sustained her as much as anything that nourished her body. . . .
>
> . . . She appreciated this daily spiritual nourishment in a new way. "I need my morning prayer even more than I need my green, leafy vegetables," she said. By seeking spiritual nourishment every day, Gwen was able to feel the Savior's sustaining presence in her life. . . .
>
> Just as properly nourishing and caring for our bodies contributes to physical well-being, caring for our spirits increases our spiritual capacities, sustains us in trials, and makes us more able to follow the Savior and accomplish our life's work.[15]

The daily nature of the "tie in" is crucial and the power it affords us cannot be underestimated. Hit or miss contact just isn't as effective.

Half-hearted effort won't cut it either. I've often asked myself, "Merrilee, which half of these blessings are you willing to give up?" I never have a good answer! I want them all! Everything the Lord is willing to give me—which is a lot! But I admit, "daily" is hard. But daily effort offers us spiritual power that is not obtained any other way.

Elder Neal A. Maxwell spoke on this subject,

> These comments are for the essentially "honorable" members who are skimming over the surface instead of deepening their discipleship and who are casually engaged rather than "anxiously engaged." (D&C 76:75; D&C 58:27.) . . .
>
> All are free to choose, of course, and we would not have it otherwise. Unfortunately, however, when some choose slackness, they are choosing not only for themselves, but for the next generation and the next. Small equivocations in parents can produce large deviations in their children! . . .
>
> One common characteristic of the honorable but slack is their disdain for the seemingly unexciting duties of discipleship, such as daily prayer, regular reading of the scriptures, attendance at sacrament meeting, paying a full tithe, and participating in the holy temples. Such disdain is especially dangerous in today's world of raging relativism and of belching sensualism, a world in which, if many utter the name of Deity at all, it is only as verbal punctuation or as an expression of exclamation, not adoration![16]

I must admit. I've read this quote many times and it gets me every time! How often am I "honorable but slack"?

In these latter days, we must "tie in" daily. Our spiritual tethering to the Lord may be the one thing that saves us in the storms that lie ahead.

Tune Out

The other day, I was sitting with the kids watching TV. It was something completely stupid. I kept saying, "This is so dumb." Time goes by. "This is such a stupid show." Times goes by. "Why am I even watching this?"

Finally, my son pipes up. "You know, Mom. You could turn it off."

It was like I woke up out of a stupor! I turned the TV off, and said to my kids, "That was a really dumb show. Let's go do something else."

That's the thing about worldliness. *We* control the power switch. We can turn it off, and we can tune it out.

Sister Julie B. Beck, general president of the Relief Society, commented on women holding this power.

> The responsibility mothers have today has never required more vigilance. More than at any time in the history of the world, we need mothers who know. Children are being born into a world where they "wrestle not against flesh and blood, but against principalities, against powers, against the rulers of the darkness of this world, against spiritual wickedness in high places" (Ephesians 6:12). However, mothers need not fear. When mothers know who they are and who God is and have made covenants with Him, they will have great power and influence for good on their children.[17]

May I add that we are *all* mothers. Whether we have children here or in the hereafter, we, by virtue of our womanhood, are all mothers. Each of us bears this responsibility and this power.

Sister Beck continues,

> Mothers who know do less. They permit less of what will not bear good fruit eternally. They allow less media in their homes, less distraction, less activity that draws their children away from their home. Mothers who know are willing to live on less and consume less of the world's goods in order to spend more time with their children—more time eating together, more time

working together, more time reading together, more time talking, laughing, singing, and exemplifying. These mothers choose carefully and do not try to choose it all.[18]

I especially love that last line: "Mothers choose carefully and do not try to choose it all." I think we fall prey to the guilt-traps that surround us when we try to choose everything, try to *do* everything. Then, when we can't do it all (because, let's be honest, we *can't* do it all, nor should we), we feel guilty. Let's toss that guilt by choosing to make wise choices.

So, what can we tune out? Now some of you might suggest that I tune out my TV. Yes, I can watch far less TV. I am clinging to the goal of "less media" in Sister Beck's talk.

We can also tune out sound. Think about how much time we have that is perfectly quiet. If you're like me, I turn on the radio (actually, the computer) and begin my day. The children hook up to their iPods. I get in the car and listen to the radio some more. Back at home in the evening, on comes the TV. And then I'm off to bed. Hardly a quiet moment.

That is why my daily walks are so precious to me. I tune out. No cell phone ringing. No radio blaring. No computer playing. No TV chattering. Quiet. Is it any wonder that I find I can hear the Spirit far more frequently during my quiet time of reflection and prayer?

Satan has been quite busy turning up the volume in our world. He knows that if he can keep our lives full of sound, it can drown out the whisperings of the still, small voice.

So think of how much quiet time you have in the day. Would you like more? Turn off and tune out. Now, if you're like me, when I turned off the radio, I was far more able to hear four little boys fighting! But how wonderful to hear the sounds of family, the sounds of life.

We can also tune out the worldly pressure to run full tilt. Recently, several young moms sat in my family room. One mom said, "My daughter really is a busy little girl. She has dance and Girl Scouts. Then she has Primary and soccer and chorus. And we're going to start her in piano. So I spend most of my time driving her around." Her daughter is eight years old. What an insane schedule! And the entire family revolves around this young child's schedule.

They are all good activities, but I thought of Elder Oaks's question, "What is best?" and wondered if perhaps it was time for that mother to pick only one activity at a time for her daughter.

Dr. William J. Doherty, a family therapist, comments on this new culture of over-commitment,

> Welcome to the strange new world where being home for dinner is a radical act. For three decades a new spiritual and social justice issue has been arising in our culture and our congregations, but we've been too busy to notice it. It's the problem of time: over-work, over-scheduling, and a chronic sense of hurry. We have become the most productive and the most time-starved people on earth. . . .
>
> . . . Parenting becomes like product development, with insecure parents never knowing when they've done enough and when their children are falling behind. . . . We are training our children to become workaholics when they grow up, in order to compete in the global economy. And parenting has become a competitive sport, with the trophies going to the busiest.[19]

Isn't that a telling commentary of our day? I can remember rushing the children and having a son ask, "Why are we in a hurry, Mom?" I couldn't answer. "I don't know, but hurry up!"

What is the rush? Why the need to over-schedule? Why are we competing on a worldly level with a worldly scorecard? Why do we care so much?

And yet we all get caught up in the swirl. We sign up for investment classes and yoga classes and a Bunko club, and we volunteer at the PTA, the PEO, and the ARC, and we have two Church callings and a full-time job, and then we wonder why we're exhausted. We might be able to do it all, but certainly not all at the same time!

So what if we take a step back and tune out? Let me suggest some things you might like to consider doing:

- Evaluate your media time and reduce the amount of time in front of the TV.
- Set aside clear times of "no noise."
- Only check e-mail at set times. (I have to turn off the e-mail program or I check it constantly! I'm like a puppy, "Yip, yip! Someone's knocking at the door! Yip, yip!")
- Question each commitment—Is this best or necessary? Will this help me meet my goals? (In fact, I use that phrase when I decline a commitment: "I'm sorry, this just doesn't meet my goals right now.")
- Evaluate the schedule of everyone in the family—including yourself—and how it impacts the family. Trim activities where necessary. Sometimes "no" just means "not now."
- Evaluate your home. Strive to reduce the prominence of media (does your TV look like a shrine?) and the amount of possessions and visual "clutter." Are there ways to increase the presence of spiritual influences instead?
- Schedule quiet time on your family calendar and *guard this time as sacred.*
- Managing our time and our choices is a constant battle. Mortality beats at the door and wants to sneak through the cracks. So I would recommend that you review this evaluation periodically.

Wonderful things happen when you tune out. You have *time!* It's amazing. And you get back your "brain space"! Relationships grow. Joy returns. All are well worth the effort to tune out!

Tap In

The third way we can be a Woman of Eternity is to attend the temple as frequently as we can. I refer to this step as "Tap in."

I was working as a receptionist in the San Diego California Temple. One evening it was rather quiet and the temple president walked by.

"Sister, how are you enjoying your service in the temple?" he asked.

"I love it," I replied. "It's clean and quiet."

He nodded thoughtfully and walked a few steps on. Then he stopped and turned back. "Sister, how many children do you have?" he asked.

"Four little boys," I responded. "And my home is rarely clean and quiet."

He burst out laughing. "Ha, ha, clean and quiet. I have to remember that." And he walked off chuckling. I'm sure others might have commented on the reverence or the spirit of the temple, but at that time, I just appreciated that I could be in a clean, quiet place for a while and take a break from the chaos of my house.

I grew up in Detroit. Michigan is maple syrup country. The maple trees are so beautiful, and they contain a wonderful surprise inside— a sweet sap that is used to make the maple syrup, which I love!

There are several important things to remember when you're making maple syrup. First, you have to tap into the *maple* tree. The oak tree, alas, just doesn't work. It's beautiful, but it does not contain the sweet maple sap inside. Neither does the sycamore tree.

When you tap into the tree, you need to hang a bucket to catch the sap. The sap flows more freely if the tree is in the sun rather than the shade. You'll also want to cover your bucket so bugs won't get into it. And it takes forty gallons of sap to make just one gallon of syrup! So you have to tap a long time to get what you want. And then the sap must be boiled within one week or it will spoil. The process sounds tricky, but the results are certainly worth the effort!

Now tapping a maple tree has many similarities to tapping into the temple. Temples of course are beautiful. But nothing compares to what is happening inside. And if we don't tap in, we'll miss out on some sweet blessings.

Part of benefiting from the temple is actually *going* to the temple. It is amazing how many excuses we can find that hinder our attendance at the temple. We think that spending time with our family or attending church is enough. But just as the oak and the sycamore are great trees, only the maple produces the true sweetness. When we go to the temple, we can tap into the ultimate spiritual power.

The sap flows more freely in the sun. The same applies to our experience in the temple. If we approach our temple attendance basking in the light of the gospel, we will get much more out of the experience. If we approach with prayer and meditation and scripture study, we will be able to tap into the deeply personal instructions from the Spirit that await us there.

Elder L. Lionel Kendrick observed,

> Our worship in the temple is in preparation to live in the presence of our Heavenly Father and His Son. . . .
>
> . . . If we can catch the vision of this eventual event, it will help us in preparing to enter His presence and in leaving the world behind as we enter His temple.[20]

In obtaining the sap, we have to guard against bugs. The same is true of our temple experience. As Elder Kendrick stated, we must leave the world behind when we enter the temple. But I believe we should also take the temple with us when we leave to reenter the world. When we take the spirit of the temple home with us, it affects our entire family. Preserving that sweet Spirit helps us enjoy the blessings of the temple longer and more deeply.

It takes a lot of sap to make syrup. So, too, it takes many experiences in the temple to yield the power and understanding that we all desire. I've been attending the temple for a long time, and I feel like I have so much more to learn! I value so much what I have gained, but I desire more.

Doctrine and Covenants 109:22 reads, "And we ask thee, Holy Father, that thy servants may go forth from this house armed with thy power, and that thy name may be upon them, and thy glory be round about them, and thine angels have charge over them." These are glorious blessings that can be ours when we attend the temple: glory, power, angels. Receiving these promises takes time and dedicated effort.

Finally, sap must be boiled within a week or it will spoil. If we are able, we must return to the temple frequently.

I think that part of the reason God wants us to go to the temple often is the same reason he called Moses and Nephi and Enoch to the mountaintop. He wanted them to see the whole picture. He wanted them to see what he sees. The same is true for us. When we go to the temple, we have a broader perspective. We see what God sees, and we go home with our vision changed and our priorities realigned.

One day many years ago, I was taking my walk and pondering the long list of community service activities I was participating in. My children were older and in school all day. I loved it because I was able to do so many wonderful things that I couldn't when they were younger. I thought of the PTA, the Boy Scouts, the Rotary Club, the Chamber of Commerce, the Red Cross, Mothers without Borders, my Church calling, and other organizations that enriched my life. I was so happy to be involved in so many wonderful things. I truly love helping people.

As I pondered all these good things, I had a thought: "What is *the most important* thing I could do to help someone else?" And the answer struck me most forcibly. The most important thing I could do for someone else was to offer them the blessings of eternity—the saving ordinances of the gospel of Jesus Christ. I had the power to do that, and it was the most desired blessing of the brothers and sisters who had passed beyond the veil.

All of a sudden, my wonderful list of good things paled in comparison. They were all good, but they were not crucial! I had been pretty faithfully attending the temple monthly, but I realized that I attended my Rotary meetings weekly! How was it I had time for one but not the other?

I committed that day that I would try to attend the temple weekly. I realized it was an ambitious goal. But I felt lucky that I lived close by a temple. I picked a morning and scheduled my temple attendance on my calendar and guarded that time zealously. I realized that I needed to trim some other activities, some other good things, which I did. ("I'm sorry. This just doesn't meet my goals right now.")

As I began to go weekly, I was filled with love for my brothers and sisters and felt so happy to be able to do this great service for them.

Then, a remarkable thing happened. It actually is hard to describe. I began to change. I found that I cared less and less for worldly things. They just didn't matter as much to me anymore. I found that when you go to the temple, you carry a "glow" with you that lingers. I found myself more patient with my family and far more understanding.

And love began to grow in my little Pharisee heart. I found myself looking at others with a far more eternal perspective— seeing them clearly as my brother or sister.

Now, if I miss a week, I feel a strange loss and cannot wait to get back.

Now each of us is in different circumstances. You may have young ones still at home. You may be a single mom with many time constraints. You may live in an area that is far from a temple.

Tapping into the temple will be different for each of us. But however we do it, as we commit to the goal of increasing and improving our temple attendance, blessings will flow. They come in a variety of beautiful ways. Women of Eternity seek these blessings, and as they sit in the temple, they know. Eternity matters. It's what this life is all about.

Tune In

Finally, after we've tied in with our daily spiritual habits, tuned out the world, tapped in to the temple, we must tune in to the Spirit.

I was speaking to some friends of mine who were discussing getting answers to prayers.

One woman asked, "How often do you get answers?"

Another was quick to respond, "Daily!"

"You're kidding me! How do you do that?"

"I pray all day long. And I ask all day long. And the answers come."

Having the Spirit guide us constantly in our lives takes work.

I'm always saying to my boys, "The Lord isn't just going to whack you over the head and say 'pay attention.' You have to ask and then listen."

Both parts take effort.

President James E. Faust described this effort,

> We must cultivate our sensitivity to that divine voice. . . .
>
> So it is with divine communication. The still, small voice, though still and small, is very powerful. It "whispereth through and pierceth all things" (D&C 85:6). . . . The message may be there but we fail to pick it up. Perhaps something in our lives prevents us from hearing the message because we are "past feeling" (see 1 Ne. 17:45).
>
> We often put ourselves in spiritual dead spots—places and situations that block out divine messages. Some of these dead spots include anger, pornography, transgression, selfishness, and other situations that offend the Spirit.[21]

As we've discussed throughout this chapter, we all have "dead spots"—worldly attitudes and behaviors that need to be eliminated. But please recognize also that these things take time. They take work, patience, and perseverance to overcome.

Tuning into the Spirit also requires that we figure out how the Spirit communicates with us individually. It is different for everyone! I have on a few occasions distinctly heard a voice in my mind. My mother has had that happen only once. My friend says she feels a warm peacefulness. Another feels tingles. Another will have a clarity of thought. I often have sudden ideas, and I think, "Wow, that's fantastic! It obviously came from the Spirit because I would have never thought of that!"

This takes trial and error to figure out. One of the ways we can increase our perception of the promptings of the Spirit is to ask! We can ask our Heavenly Father to help us identify more clearly the promptings that come to us.

It's important to seek the guidance of the Spirit all the time. My dear friend Kathy commented, "Every day, the first prayer I utter is to ask that the Lord will guide my efforts and that I will have constant direction by the Spirit." What impresses me about Kathy is that not only will she ask for that blessing, but that she will also trust the Lord to fulfill it. She absolutely and completely trusts the promptings that she feels.

> Trust in the Lord with all thine heart; and lean not unto thine own understanding.
> In all thy ways acknowledge him, and he shall direct thy paths. (Proverbs 3:5–6)

Like probably many of you, I do a lot of second guessing: "Was that me or the Spirit?" As I get older, I have learned to trust my feelings more and more. I am getting better at moving forward, confident that the direction I seek will come.

Women of Eternity tune in to the Spirit all day long. They do not wait until they have time for a formal prayer. They are in constant communication. Over time and with experience, they fine tune their ability to hear.

I believe that when we are in the presence of our Father and he plays back the video of our lives, we will be stunned to see how much we were guided by the Spirit. We will realize that we were never alone, and we will be grateful.

Each of us is working to tune out the world and focus our efforts on eternal things. Rather than feeling mired in guilt about our lack of progress, we can start fresh and anew this day and every day. Committed to improving. Committed to setting our heart on the things of eternity.

Even if we just make a little effort, the blessings of joy will begin to flow. Sweetness will be ours. And as we commit to becoming Women of Eternity, eternal joy will be ours. We don't have to wait until the hereafter to get it. That joy can be ours—here and now. The Lord is ready to bless us with unspeakable joy. All we have to do is ask.

Choosing a Better and Joyful Life

Well, now. We have approached the end of our time together. I'm thinking that going forward, we should all get together and have some really fun "Toss the Guilt" parties! We can pass around slips of paper and write down each and every thing we've been feeling guilty about. Then we could all crumple them up and play "Hit the Garbage Can." The one with the most successes could win a fat-free, sugar-free, guilt-free cheesecake! Nah, how about a fully loaded piece of cheesecake and we decide not to feel guilty about it!

I can just see parties springing up all over the place! We can wear ugly shoes and do the Worrywart salute to each other. Doesn't that sound like a load of fun? Then we can "Make a joyful noise unto God, all ye lands" (Psalm 66:1)!

Now to be honest, if you've read this far, you just might be feeling guilty about feeling guilty. And you may have generated an enormous guilt-list to add to your life. I certainly hope not!

Just remember, guilt for things other than sin is counterproductive. It wastes time and an enormous amount of emotional energy. Why bother?

Because we are women, right? We excel in guilt. So, perhaps just for this time, let's reduce our guilt load for a while. I was thinking that it's a bit like a ship at sea. Occasionally the ship has to go into port and scrape off the barnacles that have accumulated on the sides of the ship, slowing its speed. Guilt is like those barnacles.

Now I know you're thinking, "Gee, thanks, Merrilee. Now I have this horrible visual of you sitting on your chaise lounge, scraping barnacles off of your sides!" I am so sorry. It was strictly a metaphor.

We can choose to toss the guilt and not let it rule us anymore. When it creeps up, we can talk back, firmly. We can say, "Go away. I know what I need to work on, and I am doing my best. I'm not going to feel guilty anymore." Go ahead. It works. I talk to myself all the time! Sometimes, I need to give myself a good talking to!

After we toss the guilt, we are left to choose what we will use to fill its place. And we can choose to be better. We can choose a better life.

President Gordon B. Hinckley was always encouraging us.

> I speak of the need for a little more effort, a little more self-discipline, a little more consecrated effort in the direction of excellence in our lives.
>
> This is the great day of decision for each of us. For many it is the time of beginning something that will go on for as long as you live. I plead with you: don't be a scrub! Rise to the high ground of spiritual, mental, and physical excellence. You can do it. You may not be a genius. You may be lacking in some skills. But so many of us can do better than we are now doing. We are members of this great Church whose influence is now felt over the world. We are people with a present and with a future. Don't muff your opportunities. Be excellent.[1]

I loved his admonition—"Don't be a scrub!" Each of us can do better. And there is no better time to make such a commitment to be better than right now.

President Thomas S. Monson adds his voice with this important message:

Self-mastery is a rigorous process at best; too many of us want it to be effortless and painless.[2]

Truly, there is no way I can be perfect. None of us can. But we can improve a little. We can choose

- the abundant life.
- to have less guilt.
- to be better at being ourselves.
- to have a little more faith.
- to have more peace in our lives.
- to be a little more obedient.
- to be a bit stronger.
- to focus a bit more on eternity.

That we can do. These choices can happen day after day and year after year.

Being a Woman of Joy encompasses all of these choices. And what's wonderful is that we have an eternity to work on it! We don't have rigid timetables with demanding checkpoints. We can improve and choose a better life with each choice we make.

Think about this. Lehi's dream of the iron rod did not include a zip-line that a favored few could grab onto and zip right up to the tree. Every person made it the same way—step by step, hand over hand.

Sometimes that river of filthy waters will overflow our path and sweep our feet out from under us. And yes, we will hang on for dear life to the word of God until we get our footing once again. But then let us step up and begin again. Step by step.

> They did press their way forward, continually holding fast to
> the rod of iron, until they came forth and fell down and partook
> of the fruit of the tree. (1 Nephi 8:30)

Pressing forward. Continually holding fast. That we can do.

Joy is not always about the attainment—it's about the progress, and that's what our lives are about. Progress. Getting on the straight and narrow path and just sticking to it. Moving forward.

Joy comes to us like an advent calendar. Each day as we strive to be a bit better, we are rewarded with sweetness.

Joy doesn't have to wait until all the planets are aligned, and all our issues are resolved, and our behavior is perfectly executed. Joy is here for us *now.*

Frankly, joy is not wholly dependent upon us. Joy is offered to each one of us because of the atonement of the Lord Jesus Christ. He is perfect—perfect in obedience, perfect in love—and it is through him that we can receive joy.

Alma describes this joy,

> And it came to pass that as I was thus racked with torment, while I was harrowed up by the memory of my many sins, behold, I remembered also to have heard my father prophesy unto the people concerning the coming of one Jesus Christ, a Son of God, to atone for the sins of the world.
>
> Now, as my mind caught hold upon this thought, I cried within my heart: O Jesus, thou Son of God, have mercy on me, who am in the gall of bitterness, and am encircled about by the everlasting chains of death.
>
> And now, behold, when I thought this, I could remember my pains no more; yea, I was harrowed up by the memory of my sins no more.
>
> And oh, what joy, and what marvelous light I did behold; yea, my soul was filled with joy as exceeding as was my pain!
>
> Yea, I say unto you, my son, that there could be nothing so exquisite and so bitter as were my pains. Yea, and again I say unto you, my son, that on the other hand, there can be nothing so exquisite and sweet as was my joy. (Alma 36:17–21)

Sometimes we think joy has to be all complicated and drawn out. I love Alma's story because he shows how simply and immediately the joy of the Atonement can be received. We can experience this exquisite and sweet joy every day as we turn to our Savior.

King Benjamin explained this to his people,

> As ye have come to the knowledge of the glory of God, or if ye have known of his goodness and have tasted of his love, and

have received a remission of your sins, which *causeth such exceedingly great joy* in your souls, even so I would that ye should remember, and always retain in remembrance, the greatness of God, and your own nothingness, and his goodness and long-suffering towards you, unworthy creatures, and humble yourselves even in the depths of humility, calling on the name of the Lord daily, and standing steadfastly in the faith of that which is to come, which was spoken by the mouth of the angel.

And behold, even at this time, ye have been calling on his name, and begging for a remission of your sins. And has he suffered that ye have begged in vain? Nay; he has poured out his Spirit upon you, and has caused that your hearts should be filled with joy, and has caused that your mouths should be stopped that ye could not find utterance, so exceedingly great was your joy. (Mosiah 4:11, 20; emphasis added)

We have peace and love and anticipation and hope because of the Atonement. Our Savior offers us the fruit. He has paid the price. He wants us to have it. Each of us can receive it.

Wherefore, fear not even unto death; for in this world your joy is not full, but in me your joy is full. (D&C 101:36)

I testify that this joy is real. It can be ours. I have experienced it. The greatest joy in my life is to know that God lives and that he loves me. That joy surpasses all.

We are priceless daughters of God and destined for greatness. We have the power within us to be a little bit better each day. We have the power to choose a better life. And as we do so, we will also have a more joyful life. As we work to eliminate the negative influences in our lives, we will be better able to tune in to the Spirit and feel the love that is there for us.

It is my wish for you that the blessings of heaven will pour out upon you as you strive to be a better woman and have a better life and that you may catch the joy—God's joy.

"Thou hast made known to me the ways of life; thou shalt make me full of joy with thy countenance" (Acts 2:28).

Notes

Chapter 1: Women of Joy, Not Guilt

1. Victoria Gunther, "The Girl in a Whirl." Used by permission.

2. Dallin H. Oaks, "Sins and Mistakes," in *Brigham Young University 1993–94 Devotional and Fireside Speeches* (Provo, Utah: University Publications, 1994), 204.

3. Barbara Timothy Bowen, "Can I Keep These Plates Spinning?" in *An Emotional First-Aid Kit for Mothers,* ed. Linda J. Eyre (Salt Lake City: Bookcraft, 1997), 40–41, emphasis in original.

4. Dallin H. Oaks, "The Challenge to Become," *Ensign,* November 2000, 32, 34.

5. Gordon B. Hinckley, "Words of the Prophet: You Can Be Forgiven," *New Era,* October 2001, 7.

6. Anonymous. http://www.d2partners.com/januarynewsletter.html; emphasis added.

7. Gordon B. Hinckley, "Words of the Prophet: Put Your Shoulder to the Wheel," *New Era,* July 2000, 4.

Chapter 2: Women of Being, Not Comparison

1. "The Story of Goldilocks and the Three Bears." http://www.dltk-teach.com/rhymes/goldilocks_story.htm.

2. Sheri Dew, *No Doubt About It* (Salt Lake City: Deseret Book, 2001), 224, 225.

3. Merrill Christensen, "Comparing, Competing, and Individual Worth," BYU Devotional, 31 July 2007, 4, 8.

4. Ezra Taft Benson, "Beware of Pride," *Ensign,* May 1989, 4, 5.

5. Jan Underwood Pinborough, "Minerva Kohlhepp Teichert: With a Bold Brush," *Ensign,* April 1989, 35, 37–38.

6. Benson, "Beware of Pride," 6–7.

7. Dew, *No Doubt About It,* 228.

Chapter 3: Women of Faith, Not Fear

1. Norman Vincent Peale. http://www.uoflife.com/wc/concepts/thoughts3.htm.

2. John Greenleaf Whittier, "Maud Miller," in *Complete Poetical Works of John Greenleaf Whittier* (N.p.: Lovenstein Press, 2007), 151.

3. Mary Fisher, "A Whisper of AIDS: Address to the Republican National Convention," Houston, Texas, 19 August 1992. http://gos.sbc.edu/f/fisher.html.

4. Dorothy Bernard. http://www.quotationspage.com/quote/29699.html.

5. Neal A. Maxwell, *But for a Small Moment* (Salt Lake City: Bookcraft, 1986), 89.

6. Neal A. Maxwell, *That Ye May Believe* (Salt Lake City: Bookcraft, 1992), 84.

7. Joseph F. McConkie, *The Spirit of Revelation* (Salt Lake City: Deseret Book, 1984), 67–68.

8. Gordon B. Hinckley, "God Hath Not Given Us the Spirit of Fear," *Ensign,* October 1984, 2.

Chapter 4: Women of Peace, Not Worry

1. Corrie ten Boom. http://www.worldofquotes.com/topic/worry/1/index.html.

2. Author unknown. http://www.higherpraise.com/illustrations/worry.htm.

3. Edward M. Hallowell, *Worry: Controlling It and Using It Wisely* (New York: Ballantine Books, 1997), 51.

4. Gail Sheehy, *Pathfinders* (New York: William Morrow & Co., 1981).

5. "Letting Go," in *Stepping Stones to Recovery for Young People: Experience the Miracle of 12 Steps Recovery,* edited by Lisa D. (N.p.: Hazelden, 1991), 34–35.

6. Richard G. Scott, "Jesus Christ, Our Redeemer," *Ensign,* May 1997, 54.

7. Richard G. Scott, "First Things First," *Ensign,* May 2001, 7.

8. Gordon B. Hinckley, "The Things of Which I Know," *Ensign,* May 2007, 85.

9. Reinhold Niebuhr, "The Serenity Prayer." http://www.cptryon.org/prayer/special/serenity.html.

Chapter 5: Women of Obedience, Not Defiance

1. Gordon B. Hinckley, "Your Greatest Challenge, Mother," *Ensign,* November 2000, 99.

2. Gordon B. Hinckley, "Words of the Prophet: The Body Is Sacred," *New Era,* November 2006, 2, 4.

3. M. Russell Ballard, "'His Word Ye Shall Receive,'" *Ensign,* May 2001, 66; emphasis added.

4. Sheri Dew, *No One Can Take Your Place* (Salt Lake City: Deseret Book, 2004), 84.

5. Gordon B. Hinckley, *One Bright Shining Hope* (Salt Lake City: Deseret Book, 2006), 93.

6. Michelangelo. http://www.brainyquote.com/quotes/authors/m/michel angelo.html.

Chapter 6: Women of Strength, Not Weakness

1. Gordon B. Hinckley, "This Is the Work of the Master," *Ensign,* May 1995, 71.

2. From "Golda Meir," Women's International Center. www.wic.org/bio .gmeir.htm.

3. Thomas S. Monson, "First Presidency Message: In Search of an Abundant Life," *Tambuli,* August 1988, 3.

4. Dallin H. Oaks, "Our Strengths Can Become Our Downfall," *Ensign,* October 1994, 12.

5. Neal A. Maxwell, *Even As I Am* (Salt Lake City: Deseret Book, 1982), 87.

Chapter 7: Women of Eternity, Not Mortality

1. Russell M. Nelson, "The Magnificence of Man," *New Era,* October 1987, 44.

2. Connor Boyack, "A Mirror," 25 July 2007. http://africa.connorboyack .com.

3. Victor B. Cline, quoted in M. Russell Ballard, "The Effects of Television," *Ensign,* May 1989, 78.

4. Susan W. Tanner, "The Sanctity of the Body," *Ensign,* November 2005, 14–15.

5. Connor Boyack, "Smitten with Self," 15 March 2007. http://www.connor boyack.com/blog/smitten-with-self.

6. Neal A. Maxwell, "The Tugs and Pulls of the World," *Ensign,* November 2000, 35.

7. Gordon B. Hinckley, "The Times in Which We Live," *Ensign,* November 2001, 73.

8. Michael Brower and Warren Leon, "The Consumer's Guide to Effective Environmental Choices: Practical Advice from the Union of Concerned Scientists." http://www.ucsusa.org/assets/documents/ucs/CG-Chapter-1.pdf.

9. Emayzine Web site. http://www.emayzine.com/infoage/lectures/Culture_of_Real_Virtuality.htm.

10. Sacha Zimmerman, "Become a One-Television Household." http://www.rd.com/national-interest/education-issues/for-america-become-a-one-television-household/article29482.html.

11. Connor Boyack, "Gratitude," 25 November 2007. http://www.connorboyack.com/blog/gratitude.

12. Hinckley, "The Times in Which We Live," 73.

13. Dallin H. Oaks, "Good, Better, Best," *Ensign,* November 2007, 104.

14. Oaks, "Good, Better, Best," 107.

15. "The Visiting Teacher: Our Daily Bread," *Ensign,* April 1996, 43.

16. Neal A. Maxwell, "'Settle This in Your Hearts,'" *Ensign,* November 1992, 65–66.

17. Julie B. Beck, "Mothers Who Know," *Ensign,* November 2007, 76.

18. Beck, "Mothers Who Know," 77–78.

19. William J. Doherty, "Let's Take Back our Time." http://www.uuworld.org/2004/05/feature2.html.

20. L. Lionel Kendrick, "Enhancing Our Temple Experience," *Ensign,* May 2001, 79.

21. James E. Faust, "Did You Get the Right Message?" *Ensign,* May 2004, 67.

Conclusion: Choosing a Better and Joyful Life

1. Gordon B. Hinckley, "The Quest for Excellence," *Ensign,* September 1999, 4–5.

2. Thomas S. Monson, "First Presidency Message: In Search of an Abundant Life," *Tambuli,* August 1988, 3.

Index

Index